2 3 4 5 6 **7** 8 9 10

THE TECH SET

Ellyssa Kroski, Series Editor

A Social Networking Primer for Librarians

Cliff Landis

lita

Neal-Schuman Publishers, Inc.

New York   London

Published by Neal-Schuman Publishers, Inc.
100 William St., Suite 2004
New York, NY 10038

Published in cooperation with the Library Information and Technology Association, a division of the American Library Association.

Printed and bound in the United States of America.

The paper used in this publication meets the minimum requirements of American National Standard for Information Sciences—Permanence of Paper for Printed Library Materials, ANSI Z39.48-1992.

ISBN: 978-1-55570-704-0

CONTENTS

Don't miss this book's companion wiki and podcast!

Turn the page for details.

THE TECH SET is more than the book you're holding!

All 10 titles in THE TECH SET series feature three components:

1. the book you're now holding;
2. companion wikis to provide even more details on the topic and keep our coverage of this topic up-to-date; and
3. author podcasts that will extend your knowledge and let you get to know the author even better.

The companion wikis and podcasts can be found at:

techset.wetpaint.com

At **techset.wetpaint.com** you'll be able to go far beyond the printed pages you're now holding and:

▶ access regular updates from each author that are packed with new advice and recommended resources;
▶ use the wiki's forum to interact, ask questions, and share advice with the authors and your LIS peers; and
▶ hear these gurus' own words when you listen to THE TECH SET podcasts.

To receive regular updates about TECH SET technologies and authors, sign up for THE TECH SET Facebook page (**facebook.com/nealschumanpub**) and Twitter (**twitter.com/nealschumanpub**).

For more information on THE TECH SET series and the individual titles, visit **www.neal-schuman.com/techset**.

FOREWORD

Welcome to volume 7 of The Tech Set.

The coffeehouses and student centers of generations past have been replaced by today's online social networks. *A Social Networking Primer for Librarians* explains how to use today's most popular social networking Web sites to reach out to library patrons, promote your library, and build community. Social networking specialist Cliff Landis has written a stellar handbook that illustrates how to create an effective library presence within these extensive communities from project ideas, planning, and buy-in to marketing and best practices. The nuts-and-bolts of creating library pages, installing and building library applications such as catalog search boxes, creating and managing events and promotions, and using Facebook for library instruction are all outlined.

The idea for The Tech Set book series developed because I perceived a need for a set of practical guidebooks for using today's cutting-edge technologies specifically within libraries. When I give talks and teach courses, what I hear most from librarians who are interested in implementing these new tools in their organizations are questions on how exactly to go about doing it. A lot has been written about the benefits of these new 2.0 social media tools, and at this point librarians are intrigued but they oftentimes don't know where to start.

I envisioned a series of books that would offer accessible, practical information and would encapsulate the spirit of a 23 Things program but go a step further—to teach librarians not only how to use these programs as individual users but also how to plan and implement particular types of library services using them. I thought it was important to discuss the entire life cycle of these initiatives, including everything from what it takes to plan, strategize, and gain buy-in, to how to develop and implement, to how to market and measure the success of these projects. I also wanted them to incorporate a broad range of project ideas and instructions.

Each of the ten books in The Tech Set series was written with this format in mind. Throughout the series, the "Implementation" chapters, chock-full of detailed project instructions, will be of major interest to all readers. These chapters start off with a basic "recipe" for how to effectively use the technology in a library, and then build on that foundation to offer more and more advanced project ideas. I believe that readers of all levels of expertise will find something useful here as the proposed projects and initiatives run the gamut from the basic to the cutting-edge.

After listening to Cliff Landis present a talk on Facebook Apps & Libraries at the Computers in Libraries 2008 conference, I realized that the library field had a new rising star. Cliff brings his expansive knowledge and expertise to *A Social Networking Primer for Librarians*, in which he guides readers through all aspects of creating a social networking presence on behalf of their library. If you have questions about anything from proper friending etiquette to ways to blend the personal with the professional within online communities, this is the book for you.

Ellyssa Kroski
Information Services Technologist
Barnard College Library
www.ellyssakroski.com
http://oedb.org/blogs/ilibrarian
ellyssakroski@yahoo.com

Ellyssa Kroski is an Information Services Technologist at Barnard College as well as a writer, educator, and international conference speaker. She is an adjunct faculty member at Long Island University, Pratt Institute, and San Jose State University where she teaches LIS students about emerging technologies. Her book *Web 2.0 for Librarians and Information Professionals* was published in February 2008, and she is the creator and Series Editor for The Tech Set 10-volume book series. She blogs at iLibrarian and writes a column called "Stacking the Tech" for *Library Journal*'s Academic Newswire.

PREFACE

Social network sites enable libraries to pull themselves out of the dark ages of the pre-Internet era and inject themselves into the current information environment. They provide libraries with a new, exciting form of communication for reaching users and nonusers.

But, as with any innovation, fear of the unknown has fueled some libraries' resistance to change. This resistance has been compounded by debates over the usefulness and safety of social network sites such as Facebook and MySpace. Many librarians question whether spending valuable time and energy starting and maintaining such sites are worth it. Equally, many librarians don't yet understand social network sites well enough to make fully informed decisions about their potential usefulness.

A Social Networking Primer for Librarians is designed to provide a basic understanding of the tools and techniques that are available to strengthen the library–user connection. Aimed at all types and sizes of libraries, it also covers the policies and privacy applications of social network sites so that readers can make informed decisions about how to best reach their users while at the same time protecting the library's and its users' privacy and intellectual property.

▶ ORGANIZATION AND AUDIENCE

This book is organized so that readers with absolutely no previous online social networking experience can develop and maintain a social network site for their library. Chapter 1 introduces the world of social network sites, and Chapter 2 provides the tools for deciding which site to choose and how to get buy-in from administrators and coworkers. Chapter 3 covers MySpace and Facebook, from how to set up an account and navigate the site, all the way through using the sites to organize events. Readers can choose to focus on one or the other (based on which users the reader is trying to reach) or on both. Finally, advanced techniques, such as methods for creating and managing applications, for librarians with advanced skills in online social networking are included so that librarians can explore the full potential of social networking technologies.

Marketing techniques are given in Chapter 4, which provides step-by-step instructions on how to craft a winning marketing campaign using social network sites, while Best Practices are provided in Chapter 5, which includes scholarly references and research studies, as well as examples from individual libraries that are successfully using social network sites to reach library users (and potential users) in new and innovative ways. Simple methods of assessment and measurement are provided in Chapter 6, and a Glossary and Recommended Resources are also included.

A Social Networking Primer for Librarians is an excellent resource for librarians who want to increase their library's online presence, strengthen the library–patron connection through online social networks, and improve communication to boost usage.

▶1

INTRODUCTION: SOCIAL NETWORK SITE BASICS

- ▶ **Definitions and Characteristics**
- ▶ **Origin and Evolution**
- ▶ **Quick Overview of Theory**
- ▶ **Future Directions**

This chapter will provide you with a brief overview of the definitions, history, and theory behind social network sites. Librarians who explore social network sites are often met with concerns and misgivings by a variety of stakeholders. Many of these concerns are based on misinformation or out-of-date information, so this chapter will provide the background necessary to explore, build, or expand your library's presence on social networks.

▶ DEFINITIONS AND CHARACTERISTICS

Social network sites are a great way to get and stay in touch with friends, family, and associates who are spread out across the world. However, given the advances of technology in the past few years, social network sites are often a politically and emotionally charged topic for many librarians and library users. Therefore, it is important to understand what qualifies as a social network site, how they work, and what they do.

Definitions

In their paper "Social Network Sites: Definition, History, and Scholarship," boyd [*sic*] and Ellison (2007: 4) offer a clear definition of social network sites:

> We define social network sites as web-based services that allow individuals to (1) construct a public or semi-public profile within a bounded system, (2) articulate a list of other users with whom they share a connection, and (3) view and traverse their list of connections and those made by others within the system. The nature and nomenclature of these connections may vary from site to site.

The authors go on to explain that, although the term "social networking sites" is often used in general discussion, it is a misleading term. Because these sites are primarily for connecting to *existing* friends, rather than for networking with strangers, it is more appropriate to call them social network sites.

In social network sites, the central behavior is that of friending. **Friending** is the act of requesting a connection between your profile and another user's profile. When this connection is accepted by the other user, you are now considered Friends (for ease of reading, the noun form is capitalized for distinction in this book). A Friend on a social network site is not necessarily like a friend in daily life. This connection between profiles does not imply any degree of social intimacy between the two profile owners. Social network site Friends can be family, coworkers, friends, classmates, love interests, pen pals, neighbors, or any number of other relationships. This also includes friends and associates you have met solely online. This ability to friend other users allows social network site users the ability to navigate and describe their real-life social network.

Evolutions

By boyd and Ellison's (2007) definition, many sites (such as Flickr, YouTube, and Twitter) could be considered social network sites, too. Indeed, each of these sites is social in nature. However, the original goal of each of these sites was to share content in some form—photos in Flickr, videos in YouTube, and status updates in Twitter. Today, all major social network sites allow users to share photos, videos and status updates, in addition to connecting to other users. Truly, the lines continue to blur as different forms of social sites continue to add social network features.

Additionally, social network sites continue to refine the ability to friend other users. Many social network sites now allow users to add details to the relationships they have with their Friends. Users can group Friends together (people you knew in college, coworkers, etc.). In many cases, social network site users can take advantage of these groupings to ensure their privacy—I may want my close friends to be able to see my cell phone number, but I probably don't want all of my former classmates to see it.

As traditional Web sites continue to grow and change to meet the needs of their users, the sites will continue to add social elements. Examples of this can be seen everywhere, from mainstream news sites to hobbyist forums. Increasingly, visitors to traditional Web sites have the ability to interact socially by creating profiles, uploading avatars, and posting moderated comments. Librarians need to continue to be aware of and adapt to these changes, as they have already begun to strongly impact the way that we interact with users, seek information, and meet the needs of our communities. By meeting the challenges that these technological changes create, we will remain valuable and relevant to the populations that we serve.

▶ ORIGIN AND EVOLUTION

The first Web site to meet boyd and Ellison's (2007) criteria was SixDegrees.com, which started in 1997 and lasted four years. From 1997 to 2001, a series of Web sites began to include social network site features, allowing users to publically display their Friends lists. From 2002 to 2006, social network sites began to grow in number and were launched with greater speed. MySpace launched in 2003, and Facebook in 2004. By 2006, MySpace was in the lead when it became a household name via mainstream media.

The MySpace Scare

MySpace (and, to a lesser degree, other social network sites) gained a particularly bad reputation in the press in 2006. Reports began to arise of online predators preying on adolescents using the site. MySpace responded by increasing privacy options for users, deleting accounts of registered sex offenders, and working with outside groups to ensure user safety (Reuters, 2007).

During this time, Dr. Larry Rosen (2006: 5) performed two studies of MySpace with surprising results: "Most parents believe that there are many sexual predators on MySpace and that the media portrayal is accurate. Strikingly, most parents have never seen their teenager's MySpace page or their photos and do not know how much time their teen is spending on MySpace." Additionally, Rosen (2006: 2) found that teenage MySpace users were savvy in dealing with unwelcome behavior on the site: "Less than one in three have had an uncomfortable experience on MySpace but ONLY 7% to 9% were approached for a sexual liaison. Nearly all of those simply blocked the requester from contacting them through their MySpace page." Nancy Willard (2009: 1) of the Center for Safe and Responsible Internet Use backs up these conclusions: "The research demonstrates that sexual predation cases typically involve teens who willingly meet with adult men knowing they will engage in sexual activities. Deception about age or sexual intention is rare. Sexual abuse by family members and acquaintances remains a far more significant concern."

Although the risk rates for predation are exceedingly low, MySpace poses the same risks to adolescents as any other form of communication, be it telephone, e-mail, message boards, or just talking to strangers on the street. It is the responsibility of parents to teach children about the risks involved in communicating with strangers. In February 2007, a Texas judge dismissed a case where parents tried to sue MySpace after their daughter lied about her age and was sexually assaulted by a man she had met on the social network site. In his decision he wrote, "If anyone had a duty to protect Julie Doe, it was her parents, not MySpace" (Lee, 2007: C-2).

Media, Government, and Librarian Responses

The popular media's inflation of predation on MySpace was not the first of its kind. In her paper, "To Catch a Predator: The MySpace Moral Panic," Alice E. Marwick illustrates previous moral panics that have occurred surrounding child abuse, ritual sexual abuse, abduction by strangers, pedophilia, and cyberporn. As Marwick's research reveals, many of the statistics cited by legislators to back up their claims came from inflated, misinterpreted, or fabricated numbers. In comparing the case of the 1990s' cyberporn panic and the 2000s' MySpace panic, in her Introduction, Marwick (2008) writes: "Internet content legislation is directly linked to media-fueled moral panics that concern uses of technology deemed harmful to children." This can be seen in previous attempts to protect children online, including the Communications Decency Act of 1996 (which was struck down by the Supreme Court as unconstitutional in 1997), the Child Online Protection Act of 1998 (which was struck down as unconstitutional by federal courts in 2007), and the Children's Internet Protection Act of 1999 (which was upheld as constitutional in 2003).

The 2006 MySpace panic culminated in the creation of the Deleting Online Predators Act (DOPA). Similar to previous attempts to censor Internet speech, the bill aimed to restrict libraries and schools that receive E-rate funding from providing access by children and teens to "Commercial Social Networking Web sites" and "Chat Rooms." By this definition, any Web site that allows the creation of a profile, the posting of personally identifying information to that profile, and communication between profiles would be blocked. Examples include social network sites like Facebook and MySpace, as well as other sites that provide these capabilities, including Yahoo, Google, Twitter, FriendFeed, Flickr, Amazon.com, and SlashDot. It should be noted, however, that the law did not apply to non-E-rate schools and private in-home use by minors.

Librarians have traditionally been some of the loudest detractors of legislation that limits the freedom of speech rather than successfully protecting children. The American Library Association (2006) called on its members to oppose DOPA and in turn encouraged librarians and parents to use and educate themselves about social network sites, wikis, and other emerging technologies. Thanks to this intervention by librarians and other concerned parties, DOPA was never enacted as law. However, as new technologies continue to emerge, fresh challenges will be offered to the freedom of speech and information. Librarians will no doubt be on the forefront of protecting those freedoms.

▶ QUICK OVERVIEW OF THEORY

Social network sites quickly became a popular subject of study in academic circles, in large part because of their viral popularity. Sociologists, psychologists, computer scientists, and, of course, library scientists have all become fascinated with social network sites as the subjects of study and locations for research deployment. This body of research has brought together a variety of information sources to explain our rapidly growing use of these sites, as well as what they say about our social and cultural lives.

Humans Are Social

Social network sites are popular because they capitalize on human nature. As social creatures, we want to know what is happening to the people we care about. We learn new and interesting things from our colleagues and experts within our field. We meet new individuals with similar interests through introduction by friends. All of these social interactions (and many more) are taking place in a virtual environment through social network sites.

This social nature is likely part of our biology. Anthropologist Robin Dunbar studied the size of the neocortex in primates and found that it correlated to the number of stable relationships that one could mentally maintain. This number, 147.8, is commonly rounded up to 150. Therefore, according to Dunbar's (1993) Rule of 150, we can mentally maintain stable relationships with approximately 150 individuals. However, with the advent of social network sites (and the Internet in general), we are able to extend the number of connections that we can maintain. Although I may not keep in daily contact with my middle-school biology teacher, I can use sites like MySpace or Facebook to maintain a connection with that individual and continue to remain informed about his or her life.

It is a common concern raised by librarians and parents alike that social network sites lead to a decrease in interaction in "meaningful, local, face-to-face" relationships. In contrast, a study of Toronto's "Netville," where Internet access was ubiquitous and easily available, found that constant access to the Internet changed and improved neighbor relations when combined with online discussion boards:

> The Internet especially supports increased contact with weaker ties. In comparison to non-wired residents of the same suburb, more neighbors are known and chatted with, and they are more geographically dispersed around the suburb. Not only did the Internet support neighboring, it also facilitated discussion and mobilization around local issues. (Hampton and Wellman, 2003: 1)

Similarly positive results were found by Ellison, Steinfield, and Lampe (2007). In a discussion of college students' social capital, they found that Facebook usage had a strong correlation to an increase in bridging and bonding capital, as well as maintained social capital—the ability to stay connected to individuals one knew through previous communities.

Adults versus Teens

Reports in the media and the work of policymakers often focus on children and teenagers when discussing social network sites. And yet recent studies have shown that adults make up a majority of social network site users.

In "Adults and Social Network Web Sites," a report of the Pew Internet & American Life Project, Amanda Lenhart (2009) reveals that adult usage of social network sites has quadrupled from 2005 to 2008, with 35 percent of online adults having a profile on a social network site. In comparison, 65 percent of online teens have a social network site profile; however, because there are more adults than teens in the United States, adults currently make up the majority of social network site users. It should be noted, however, that most of these adults are younger adults, aged 18–34. These adults are primarily using social network sites to stay in touch with friends and to plan social activities with friends.

An earlier study of the social network site behavior of teens reveals a contrast to the adults. The percentage of online teens who have a social network site profile has risen 10 percent in the past two years. Older girls are the most likely group to have used a social network site. Girls are also more likely to use the site to maintain current friendships, whereas teenage boys are more likely to use social network sites to flirt or to meet new people (Lenhart and Madden, 2007).

These differences by age group and sex reveal the diverse ways in which people use social network sites. It is a mistake to stereotype any technology as being used by only a certain segment of the population. As social network sites continue to spread in use, libraries will need to utilize the advantages that they offer to serve a diverse population.

Identity

Social network sites also allow users to engage in impression management. This is first done by the selection of Friends. Users are able to judge other users by the company they keep; by friending individuals, users describe their social circle. Social network sites like Facebook increase this discernment by stating how many mutual friends users have among them. As your social network is described, it can change the way that other users perceive you (boyd, 2006). If you are a librarian who is only Friends with other librarians, not with any users, it sends a message to both librarians and users alike that you are not interested or not able to be Friends with users.

Social network site users will also friend institutions, companies, public figures, and fictional characters as a form of identity performance. In Facebook, people are represented with **Profiles**, while institutions are represented with **Pages**, which users can then become Fans of. College Facebook users, for example, may become Fans of their university, sorority, and library. This shows not only that the user is interested or happy with these organizations but also that they "belong" to the group of people who are also Fans. This group membership helps the user to identify others with common interests and also declares to those viewing his or her profile that the user is a part of this community.

In gathering Friends on social network sites, the librarian builds up a potential "imagined audience" for all of the photos, videos, wall posts, status updates, and other new content placed on the library's Web site:

> On MySpace, an individual's perceived audience frames the situation. . . . [Cultivating an imagined audience] is a practice that is commonplace for people like writers and actors who regularly interact with the public through mediating technologies. Without having cues about who will witness a given expression, an imagined audience provides a necessary way of envisioning who should be present. The size and diversity of this imagined community depends on the individual; some imagine acquiring fans while others imagine a community that is far more intimate. (boyd, 2007: 14)

For librarians, this imagined audience should be the library's users (rather than other librarians). By writing to our library's users, we are letting them know that they are the reason that we do the work that we do.

▶ FUTURE DIRECTIONS

By looking at past trends in technology and business, we can see some of the directions in which social network sites will grow in the future. To attract more users, major social network sites are currently trying to reach out to international markets. Social network sites gain more value as more people join. Therefore, in an increasingly global world, it is important for these sites to take advantage of the global social connections that their users have.

Social network sites are also trying to gather new users by providing more services. With the growing emphasis on mobile computing, both MySpace and Facebook began offering "Lite" views of their Web sites, allowing dial-up and mobile users to access core features without all the glitter and flash that can slow down the loading of pages. Also, shortly after Twitter gained speed as a microblogging tool, Facebook and MySpace enhanced their services to include the ability to perform status updates via mobile devices like cell phones (O'Neill, 2009). Similar mimicry can be seen in the creation of classifieds, in competition with sites such as Craigslist, or photo sharing, in competition with Flickr or Picasa. As new technological and networking services catch on with the populace, major social networks will scramble to mimic the service.

Given the widespread usage of social network sites, it is likely that Facebook and MySpace will both be around for some time, in one form or another. However, given the dramatic growth in technological innovation, it won't be long before some new social tool sweeps the world, and librarians will scramble to provide excellent service to users in another new format!

▶2

PLANNING

▶ **Choose a Social Network Site**

▶ **Make the Proposal and Get Buy-In**

▶ **Encourage Staff and User Involvement**

▶ **Keep Up with Changes**

Taking the time to plan is vital to the success of implementing any new library technology, such as social network sites. By thinking ahead about the benefits and drawbacks of creating a library presence in a social network site, you can anticipate any problems you may encounter. Planning will also allow you to craft a library presence that will meet your users' needs rather than just replicating what other libraries have done.

▶ CHOOSE A SOCIAL NETWORK SITE

With the proliferation of social networks on the Web, it can seem like a daunting task to choose which social network site to focus on. This section will give you the tools necessary to choose which site will be the best investment of time and energy in order to reach your library's users.

Go Where Your Users Are

There are several techniques that you can use to quickly assess which social network sites your users are actively using. One of the easiest is to search the site itself; almost all social network sites allow users to search by geographic area. Doing a quick search for your service area on each site will allow you to assess how many potential users you can reach with each site.

You can also include a quick poll on your library's Web page using software like SurveyMonkey (www.surveymonkey.com) or AdvancedPoll (www.proxy2.de/scripts.php). When polling users, explain in a few sentences why the library is interested in having a presence on a social network site; this will help to allay any initial knee-jerk reactions. Also, make sure to ask which sorts of services they would like to see included in the library's profile on a social network site—in addition to giving you more data for focusing your service, it also educates your users about the possibilities that social network sites offer. But know ahead of time that a few of your users may reveal that they would not be interested in a library presence in a social network site. For this reason, it is helpful to include an open text box in any poll for users to provide additional thoughts and opinions.

MySpace

From 2006 to mid-2008, MySpace dominated the social network site world. It quickly gained popularity among teens and young adults as a place to share and discover music, with several current mainstream artists having gotten their start through MySpace. Once it started growing, the social network site garnered an adult following, and, as of 2006, over half of its users were over 35 years of age (comScore, 2006). Although it has been surpassed in daily usage by Facebook, MySpace still has a strong following. MySpace is covered in detail in Chapter 3.

Facebook

Facebook is currently the largest social network site on the Web, ranking fourth most visited of all Internet sites (Alexa Internet, 2009). What started as a Harvard-only social network site was soon opened to other universities, then a separate site was created for high schools, and finally Facebook was opened to the public. Facebook surpassed MySpace in April 2008, but this dominance is not guaranteed in the long run. Facebook is also covered in detail in Chapter 3.

Friendster, Hi5, Orkut, and Other Social Network Sites

Although MySpace and Facebook are the most commonly known social network sites in the United States, they are by no means the only ones. Many users belong to multiple social network sites in order to connect with different Friends, and different social circles often use different social network sites to stay in touch.

MySpace and Facebook are popular around the world, but other social network sites often have a particular strength in specific geographical areas. For example, Hi5 (http://hi5.com) is the social network site of choice in Jamaica, while Orkut (www.orkut .com) is particularly popular in Brazil. Librarians in the United Kingdom should first check out Bebo (www.bebo.com), while librarians in Asia might be better off exploring Friendster (www .friendster.com). Librarians should be aware of the prevalent social networks in their geographic regions to ensure that they are not only investing their time and energy wisely but also that they will effectively reach the users in their area.

Social networks are also known to change demographics. Friendster started as a San Francisco Bay area social network in 2002 but has become popular in Asia in the past few years. As company leadership, technology, site features, and users' needs change, each social network site's success and user populations will change.

Subcultures: Artists, Lawyers, Genealogists, etc.

Librarians who serve specific communities will want to engage members of those communities through their natural online hang-out places. Librarians at fine arts colleges should check out Call for Creativity (www.callforcreativity.com), MyArtSpace (www. myartspace.com), and QuarterLife (www.quarterlife.com) as ways to connect with users and find out what they need. Law librarians will find a welcome place at LawLink (www.lawlink.com), while medical librarians may be interested in sites like Patients Like Me (www.patientslikeme.com) or RareShare (http://rareshare .org). Genealogy librarians should be aware of Kincafe (http://kincafe .com) and Famiva (http://famiva.com), social network sites organized around genealogy and family trees.

For other topics of interest, it is always possible to meet groups of interested parties via Meetup (http://meetup.com). Groups of Meetup users will gather in person to discuss or participate in hobbies, interests, and pastimes. For every hobby or interest out there, there is a Web 2.0 hangout for those interested in it. Getting to know your particular community will allow you to interact with them naturally—through the social network sites they already use.

Business/Professional Development: LinkedIn, Ning, etc.

Several social network sites are designed specifically for professionals. These sites allow professionals in various fields (including librarianship!) to network, get help with problems, perform job searches, and learn from others in their field.

LinkedIn is the most wide-reaching social network of its kind (www.linkedin.com). It is used by job-seekers to find available positions, learn about potential coworkers, and view the skills and experiences of peers in their field. To get the most out of LinkedIn, it is important to complete your profile in detail. LinkedIn allows you not only to list your education and experience but also to provide an executive summary of your skills, a list of specialties that you have within the field, and recommendations that you have from coworkers, former employers, and contacts.

Ning is a Web site that allows users to design their own social network sites. For example, the Library 2.0 Ning (http://library20 .ning.com) provides a space for librarians to learn about and discuss Library 2.0 developments and technologies. Ning is a great way to explore different avenues of professional development and connection. Additionally, some libraries are using Ning as a way to connect their users with each other (Stephens, 2009).

ALA Connect is the American Library Association's own social network site (http://connect.ala.org). ALA members are automatically signed up for the service and can log in using their ALA username and password. Users can work collaboratively with members of their Roundtables, Divisions, Committees, and Sections, or they can create community-based groups to explore library-related topics. Members of these groups can share documents, participate in discussion boards, vote on polls, and chat in real time.

Web Sites with Social Features: Flickr, YouTube, etc.

Libraries have made use of a variety of social media to connect with their users. Although not strictly social network sites, many Web sites include the basic elements of a social network: the abilities to create a profile, friend other users, and view users' Friend lists.

Flickr, the photo sharing site (www.flickr.com), is popular with libraries for sharing photos and short videos of events and services. YouTube (www.youtube.com) allows many libraries to reach their users with quick videos. Contests for user-created videos have given many libraries fresh new advertisements for their services. Many libraries (and librarians) are using Twitter (http:/twitter.com), a microblogging Web site, for marketing, outreach, and just staying in touch with users and librarians. Delicious (http://delicious .com), a social bookmarking Web site, makes collecting and searching authoritative Web links much easier for both librarians and users. These and many other Web 2.0 services are making it easier for users to connect with the library and their librarians.

▶ MAKE THE PROPOSAL AND GET BUY-IN

Although many librarians may be interested in new and emerging technologies, there is often the worry that presenting anything new or technology based will be met with resistance and fear by fellow librarians, administrators, and staff. However, a little careful planning can help you present social network sites (or any new technology) in a positive light while still being honest about its potential drawbacks.

Administrators

When presenting an initial proposal to use social network sites at your library, it is important to:

1. Include data
2. Tell stories
3. Dispel fears

Including data gives the administrator solid numbers on which to judge the merit of the proposal. While gathering and presenting data is a lot easier than it first sounds, there are a variety of quantitative information sources that can be used to justify your proposal. Start by pulling together demographic data for your area, library usage statistics, and any previous assessments your library has done. You can include national or international statistics for social network site usage, but remember that you want to focus on *your library's* users. Join the social network site you are interested in utilizing, and do a quick search to see how many users are in your service area for each social network site.

In addition to presenting data, it is important to tell stories about your library's users and the experiences of other libraries to show that the proposal is about more than just "keeping up" with technology or trends. Any library with a public workstation will have seen a social network site in action more than once. When interacting with library users, casually ask them if they use a social network site, and, if so, what they like about it. If you poll users through the library's Web site, be sure to include a text box so that they can tell the library what interests them about the service. See if other libraries similar to yours already have a social network profile, and ask them about their experiences and the reactions of their users. By gathering the stories of your users and similar users at other libraries, you can show the customer service value that a social network site can add.

Last, it is important to anticipate and address problems when presenting a proposal to administrators in order to dispel fears. Questions about security, cost, time investment, user and staff attitudes, public image, training, and assessment should all be thought about and discussed in the proposal. Again, contacting similar libraries and asking about their experiences will be invaluable in discovering potential problems and solutions. By addressing these problems at the outset, you will begin to reduce those fears the administration may have about social network sites.

Staff

Because staff members deal directly with the public on a daily basis, they are keenly aware of the way that people use the library (and how they *think* people should use the library). Staff need the same kinds of information that administrators do. Several tips will help when trying to get buy-in from staff.

In addition to presenting data and stories to staff, be ready to dispel their additional fears. Casual conversations with library staff will reveal their interest or skepticism about using social network sites to reach out to users. Some staff may be concerned about how it will impact their workload, as well as whether it is "appropriate" for libraries to be present in these spaces. Often these same staff members will never have had any firsthand exposure to social network sites. Give them time to explore other libraries' MySpace profiles or Facebook pages and ask questions. Ask them what *they* would like to see on a library's profile. By emphasizing the human, social nature of the library, you can show that increasing outreach through these spaces allows users of all ages, backgrounds, and levels of library experience to get help exploring the library.

Louise Alcorn, Reference Technology Librarian at West Des Moines Public Library, discovered that staff members have a diverse range of comfort with social network sites:

> I'd wanted to create a social networking presence for the library for some time, but was waiting for better staff buy-in. Our teen area assistant, quite reasonably, kept asking why we didn't have Facebook and Twitter up yet, as she'd created a Facebook page (on her own) for the library, for her Teen Advisory Group to "friend." However, it was attached to her personal account and she wanted to disentangle them. I agreed. Ultimately, I waited until a few nearby libraries, of similar type and composition to ours, had Facebook and Twitter set up, then said "now is the time." By then it was seen as an inevitability, and I could proceed. If I had it to do all over again, I'd do it YEARS sooner, and I'd be more proactive with getting staff involved. (Alcorn, personal communication, October 19, 2009)

Alcorn learned firsthand of the staff buy-in necessary to make the library's social network site a success. However, once the library's presence was established, she also took the initiative to integrate the library's Facebook and Twitter accounts to make library users' experience better:

> We're largely repeating our existing News items, but this way, they can follow us on their home Twitter feed or their phone, so it comes to them. They don't have to remember to check the library website, though we do use the feed to drive traffic there. It's still early, but since our Facebook Page cost us nothing (unlike our website), I'd call it a success even if only a few people followed us—and we've easily got over 60 followers just in about a month. (Alcorn, personal communication, October 19, 2009)

For more tips on getting buy-in, see Chapter 7 of Michael Stephens' (2006) *Web 2.0 & Libraries: Best Practices for Social Software.*

▶ ENCOURAGE STAFF AND USER INVOLVEMENT

Implementation of your library's presence on a social network site should be approached as an ongoing, evolving project. Do not get hung up on trying to make everything "perfect," but instead see it as a growing conversation that you're having with your library's users. You must continually advertise your services to reach new users (covered in Chapter 4: Marketing). As your library changes to meet the needs of users and to accommodate the growth of technology, your library's profile should reflect this.

Management

The first question many librarians ask when they consider a social network site presence for their library is about time investment: How much time will I have to take away from my already busy schedule to keep up with this? In general, social network sites require an initial setup time of about 5 to 15 hours, depending on the familiarity of the librarian with the site. After the initial time investment, however, maintenance may only require 15 to 30 minutes each week. Most sites allow for e-mail notifications, enabling the librarian to check his or her e-mail to see if anything on the site needs attention.

In many libraries, the social network site profile is managed and updated by one or two dedicated individuals with an interest in this type of technology. However, general staff members should be involved at every stage of planning and implementation. It is best to have a "vertical team" that includes members of every level of library hierarchy (from volunteer shelvers to administration) as well as library users. This diversity will help the social network site profile reflect the library as it truly is—a community space made up of a wide variety of people. This range of perspectives also prevents the profile from speaking to only one type of library user. Additionally, having staff from all over the library involved prevents internal anxiety that one or two tech-savvy library workers are conspiring in secret to speak on behalf of the whole library.

If you are building a teen-specific profile or page, get input from regular library users, but also try to reach teens who aren't regular library users—see what they are looking for from their library, and find out why they don't already use it. You might be surprised at the responses!

Additionally, as part of the planning process, it is important to consider the long-term challenges of managing a social network site presence. Robin Hastings, Information Technology Coordinator at Missouri River Regional Library, discovered this firsthand:

> I didn't set up our original Facebook Page, it was set up with another staff member as an administrator. When that staff member left the library, we had a very hard time transitioning to me as the main admin of the page. I eventually asked that former staff person to remove the page altogether and created the page over using a former library supporter's name as the personal account. This way, if I ever leave the library, someone else can take over that personal account and continue to manage the library's page without interruption. We have almost recovered from the loss of our previous page, though, and don't seem to have suffered too much from the problem. (Hastings, personal communication, October 15, 2009)

Hastings was able to successfully recover from this challenge by being innovative and adaptable. By planning early for inevitable transitions you can prevent similar challenges from arising for future administrators of the library's social network site presence.

Policies

Some teams may find it helpful to write a Social Media Policy for their library. This document can serve as a guide for the creation and management of content, as well as providing a written vision for the use of social media. Examples of company, nonprofit, and governmental organizations' policies can be found at the Online Database of Social Media Policies (http://socialmediagovernance .com/policies.php).

Additionally, the Social Media Policy should address user behavior on the library's social media sites. This will ensure that patrons are aware of any restrictions on their use of the library's social network sites and other social media. An excellent example of this is Ottawa Public Library's Social Media Policy (www.biblioottawalibrary .ca/files/OPL%20social%20media%20policy.pdf).

Implementation and Project Ideas

When planning your library's social network site presence, consider what sort of services you would like to offer in this space. These are some services that libraries have provided:

- ▶ Subject guides
- ▶ Instruction
- ▶ Acquisition suggestions
- ▶ Marketing
- ▶ Catalog/database searches
- ▶ Chat services
- ▶ Reference discussion boards
- ▶ Online book clubs
- ▶ Outreach
- ▶ Reader's advisory

However, do not feel limited by these suggestions. The best new services are always created by users who voice a need and librarians who rise to that challenge!

User-Driven versus Librarian-Driven Profiles

Librarians are control freaks, by nature. We're used to information control, controlled vocabulary, and strict hierarchies of organization. However, the advent of Web 2.0 has revolutionized the way that we can work collaboratively with our library users to manage information. Social network sites are a great way to see how users can imagine and describe their library.

The traditional librarian approach to any project is for a leader to have strict overall control and for smaller jobs to be delegated to committee members or underlings. This technique might work for the social network sites, but it usually ends up with a profile that is cold, static, and inhuman. By allowing the library's profile to be constantly evolving, quick with updates and (dare I say it?) less than perfect, you will reach out to users in a timely and effective manner. This is better than trying to make sure that everything is perfect and therefore delaying the release of information or, worse yet, stopping it altogether.

Another great way to encourage the use of your library's presence on social network sites is to put the profile in the hands of the user. At academic libraries, putting the library's profile in the hands of a student worker will often ensure that the students' information needs are being met on time, as well as ensuring that the profile appeals to students. The same technique works in public libraries, where it can be particularly effective for teen outreach programs. One of the first to do this was Aaron Schmidt at Thomas Ford Memorial Library (Western Springs, IL), who put the library's MySpace profile in the hands of the teen advisory board (Houghton-Jan, 2006). Teenagers know what is hot and what will reach others their age. In many cases, teens are thirsting for responsibility and would love the opportunity to show their skills and abilities by managing a library's public presence on a social network site.

Regardless of who manages the library's presence, that presence should be monitored but not controlled! Micromanagement of social site projects will quickly pull the fun right out of them, turning them into one more dull, boring task that "has to be done." The power behind social network sites, the connection with other users, is what makes them fun, interactive, and a great place to experiment! Keep encouraging those who work on the site, reminding them to find new and innovative ways to reach out to users and to help them find the information they need.

▶ KEEP UP WITH CHANGES

Social network sites are constantly changing to keep up with emerging technologies and the needs of their users. Librarians should do the same so as not to be caught off guard. First, subscribe to the site's official blog—any major changes to software, upcoming features, changes to terms of service, or service outages will be reported via the blog. Additionally, you can subscribe to site-specific news at Mashable (www.mashable.com), a third-party news site that reports on social media. By being aware of changes before they happen, you can adjust your library's social network services early rather than merely reacting to change after it has happened.

▶3

IMPLEMENTATION

▶ **Create a MySpace Account**

▶ **Create a Facebook Account**

▶ CREATE A MYSPACE ACCOUNT

MySpace emerged quickly in 2006 to dominate the social network landscape. It became famous for being popular with high school students and for being a venue for the discovery of new bands. As of February 2009, MySpace's user base is much more diverse, with 41.19 percent being 35 years old or older (Watershed Publishing, 2009). Librarians were some of the earliest adopters of MySpace and have used the site in a variety of ways to reach out and provide service. This section will show you how to set up a MySpace account for yourself or your library and will walk you through the steps necessary to create and manage OpenSocial applications in MySpace.

Getting Started

Signing up for a MySpace account is simple:

1. Click on the "Sign Up!" tab on the MySpace homepage (www.myspace.com).

2. Enter your e-mail address, a password, your full name (or the name of your library if you're setting up an institutional account), your date of birth, and your gender.

3. Read through the Terms of Service and Privacy Policy, and then click on "Sign Up!"

4. Fill in the security test (to ensure that you are not creating spam), and confirm your e-mail address to prevent spam.

Setting Up Your Account and Profile

Once you have confirmed your e-mail address, you will be asked for three types of information to help you get started with MySpace. First, it will ask you to upload a photo, which will allow Friends to positively identify you. Next, you will be asked to add a school, which allows you to reconnect with schoolmates based on your graduating class. Last, MySpace will ask you to enter a location to help you locate nearby Friends. Although you can skip each of these steps, completing them at the beginning will help you connect with your Friends.

As you get more comfortable with the MySpace interface, you can add additional customizations to your profile. MySpace allows you to create a unique, direct **MySpace URL** for your profile. This URL will make it easier for your Friends to locate you and will also make it easier to share your profile with users. For example, my personal profile URL is http://myspace.com/clifflandis (a simple and descriptive URL is best).

One of the perks of MySpace is the ability to customize the overall look of your profile. This is an excellent way to create a library brand by tying in the visual appearance of your library's MySpace profile with the library's Web page. Begin by choosing "Customize Profile" from the "Profile" drop-down menu. It is simple to choose from the available themes to begin customizing your profile. If you are familiar with HTML and CSS (cascading style sheets), you can tweak the templates or design your own. For more on this topic, see Chapter 4, "Marketing."

Connecting with Friends

Making connections with Friends is the heart of social networks. Your **Friends** (spelled with a capital F) could be coworkers, friends, family members, acquaintances, library users, or even folks you've met online who share many of your interests. By **friending** these users, you are creating a connection between your two profiles, which shows that you know each other in some form.

You will notice that when you created your MySpace account, you already had one Friend—Tom, the founder of MySpace! Now you can locate your Friends in several ways. First, click on the "Find Friends" link, and you will see that it gives you the option to import your address book from your Gmail, MSN, or AOL e-mail program. You can also search for individuals by name or e-mail. Additionally, you can browse through users based on school affiliation, interest, or career. As you add Friends, MySpace will identify potential Friends based on common connections and suggest them to you.

As you search or browse through users, you will be able to click on the users' names to view their profiles. You can also add each user as a Friend or send him or her a message. It is generally a good idea to send an introductory message to users you have not talked to before friending them. For more on friending etiquette, see Chapter 5: Best Practices.

Staying in Touch: Mail, Status and Mood, IM, Groups, and Comments

Several tools built into the MySpace Web site allow for easy communication with Friends. **Mail** is similar to e-mail, allowing users to send private one-on-one messages to each other. Messages can be sent by going to a user's page and clicking on "Send Message" or by clicking on "Mail" from the toolbar at the top of the screen.

Status and Mood allows you to post what you are doing and how you feel at the moment. This is a great way to emphasize the humanity of the library and library staff. If your institution has a profile, feel free to create statuses and moods for the library as a whole (such as "Staying open late to help students with midterms. Feeling: tired."). This is also a great way to communicate your own feelings and daily activities as an individual librarian.

MySpace's **instant messaging** (IM) service allows for private one-on-one communications between Friends. You can enable this service by downloading and installing the MySpace IM program, or you can add your MySpace IM information to a chat aggregator program like Pidgin, Meebo, or Trillian. Don't be surprised if your library's patrons use this service occasionally to pop in and ask for help!

Groups are a great way to stay in touch with other users with similar interests, groups of colleagues, or people in the same course. Students have used groups to study collectively (with group names like "Indiana University Library Students' Group"), while other users use groups to proclaim their identity by associating themselves with a group (such as "Glendale [AZ] Public Library Teen Group" or "Irving Public Library Anime Club").

You can write **Comments** on your Friends' profiles. A comment allows you to leave a message that is publicly viewable to anyone who visits that person's profile. This could be the general public or only that user's Friends, depending on the privacy settings. Comments are a great way to say hello, wish someone a happy birthday, offer condolences, or have a quick public conversation.

Showing Off: Pictures, Videos, Songs, Bulletins, and Blogs

One of the features that draws users to social network sites is the ability to share media, and MySpace is no exception. Users can share **Pictures** with each other, group photos into albums, and tag other MySpace users in their photos. If you have an institutional profile, don't forget that you can tag your building in students' photos—this is a great way to draw users to your profile!

Videos are another great way to show off the library. By sharing videos of past events, reviews of resources, or even user-designed advertisements, you can quickly begin to pull in new users. You can record videos directly from a Webcam or upload small video files (smaller than 512 MB).

Users can add **Songs** to their profile, allowing them to advertise their favorite song of the moment. MySpace has become a way for small bands to get a lot of publicity outside of the mainstream; several current stars got their start on MySpace. There's always fun music to add to your library's profile, such as the parody punk band Harry and the Potters (www.myspace.com/harryandthepotters)!

Bulletins are a way to make short posts that are viewable to all your Friends. They are a popular feature with MySpace users for filling out quizzes, making announcements, advertising events, and asking for help from the community at large. Bulletins are a good way to get to know your Friends, as well as advertise your library's services.

In addition to bulletins, MySpace has built-in **Blogs**. These blogs allow for more in-depth coverage of content and provide additional information (such as your mood when you wrote the content). Users will see the title of your blog posts on your profile, and they can also subscribe to your blog posts to receive e-mail notifications when you post new content.

Choosing Privacy Settings

As experts in the world of information, librarians are already aware of privacy concerns. However, in recent years, we have been pleasantly surprised to see many social network site users respond to threats to their privacy with equal fervor. You can adjust your privacy settings by clicking on the "My Account" link from the main menu. Pay close attention to the "Privacy," "Spam," "Notifications," "Applications," "MySpaceID," and "Miscellaneous" sections, as each one has privacy options. These options include limiting what others can see on your profile, limiting who can send you messages, and limiting how often you receive e-mails from MySpace. Some librarians feel comfortable providing a great deal of access to MySpace (such as revealing their personal contact information on MySpace), while others do not. If you are unsure about your comfort level, err on the side of caution and don't enter the information—you can always go back and add more information as you become more comfortable with the service.

Adding HTML Widgets and MySpace Applications

There are two ways to include additional content on MySpace (such as your library's catalog search or chat service). The first way is to include an HTML widget. This is a chunk of code that you put in your profile to have the desired effect. An example of this would be to place a chunk of code that allows a visitor to your profile to search your library's catalog. The Ann Arbor District Library uses this in the "About Me" section of its profile (www.myspace.com/annarbordistrictlibrary). Because this code is placed directly into the profile, users must visit that profile to access the catalog search (see Figure 3.1).

▶ Figure 3.1: Ann Arbor District Library's (AADL) Catalog Search

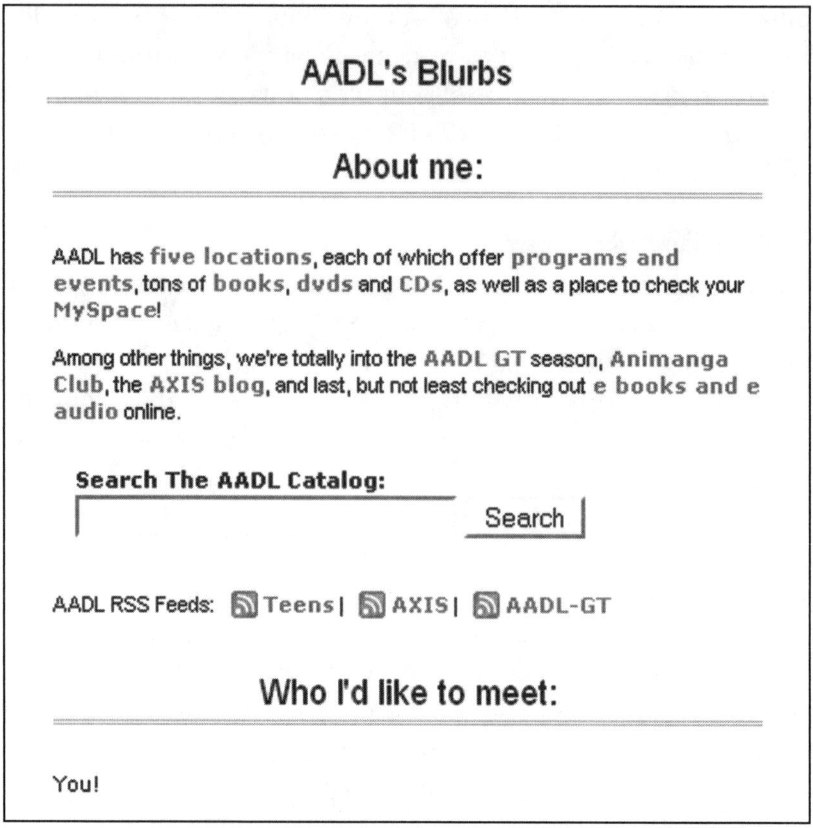

The second way to include additional information on MySpace is to install a MySpace application. Applications are user-created programs that are housed within the MySpace platform. There are a wide variety of applications available, with the majority being social or entertainment applications (this should come as no surprise because social networks are primarily social spaces). This chapter will show you how to work with HTML widgets and MySpace applications, how to create your own MySpace application, and how to manage applications you create.

Finding, Installing, and Managing Applications

You can find applications by clicking on "More" from the main menu and selecting "Apps Gallery" (see Figure 3.2). You can then search the gallery by name or browse through the categories to lo-

▶ Figure 3.2: Apps Gallery

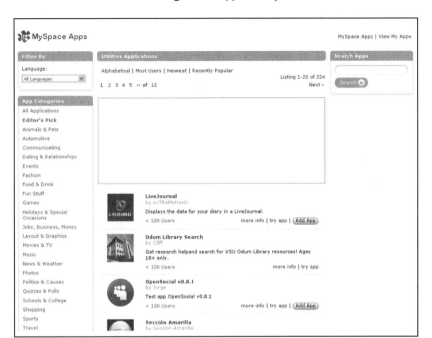

Top 5 Most Popular Apps

According to the MySpace site (http://apps.myspace.com/ Modules/AppGallery/Pages/index.aspx?fuseaction=apps&st= totalinstalls), the following are the most popular apps (as of December 16, 2009):

- ▶ Mobsters
- ▶ Mafia Wars
- ▶ Own Your Friends!
- ▶ Truth Box
- ▶ Zynga Poker

---

cate applications. For each application, you can click on the application's title, icon, or "More Info" to see more information about that application. You can also click on the "Try App" link to view that application's **Canvas page**. The canvas page is the application's home on MySpace, and it allows you to use the application without adding it, if possible (some applications must be added to your profile before they can work). Once you find an application that you wish to add, click on "Add App." MySpace will then confirm where you would like the app to be added. You can add the application to your **Homepage** so that you can see it whenever you use MySpace. You can also add the application to your **Profile page** so that other users can see the application when they visit your profile. Additionally, you can choose to have changes to the application advertised to your Friends. This way, Friends can see when you add, update, or change the application.

Many applications use personal information that you supply to MySpace, such as your name, location, age, and display photos. Although most applications require some basic information, other applications may request additional information such as public photos or videos or the songs you have added to your profile. Also, some applications may send you messages or comments. You can adjust all these settings by selecting "Profile" from the main menu and clicking on "My Apps." This will take you to the applications settings page where you can adjust these options. It is strongly advised that you look at an application's settings immediately after adding the application so that you can avoid unnecessary messages or releasing private information.

Adding Chat Reference Widgets and Applications

Many libraries provide IM, chat, or texting (SMS) services. Integrating these services into your library's MySpace profile can be a powerful way to spread the reach of these services to more people. Various programs are used to provide these services, including AOL Instant Messenger, Yahoo Messenger, Windows Live Messenger, Jabber, and Google Talk. In addition, many libraries use chat aggregators (such as Pidgin, Adium, Trillian, Meebo, and Fire) to combine all of their chat service programs (including MySpace IM) into a single interface. Libraries can also use widgets that embed chat services into their libraries' pages. These widgets (such as LibraryH3lp, MeeboMe, AIM Wimzi, Plugoo, and various other services) make it possible for users to chat with a librarian without downloading or installing software and without having to set up any accounts.

Because MySpace pages can be edited using HTML and CSS code, librarians can install chat widgets directly into their profiles. For example, the Library Loft of Charlotte & Mecklenburg County (www.myspace.com/libraryloft) uses the MeeboMe widget in the "About Me" section of their MySpace profile so that visitors to the profile can chat with librarians directly whenever they are online.

A variety of instant messaging and chat applications have been built for MySpace. For example, users can add the MySpace IMe application, and visitors to that user's profile will be able to chat directly with the profile owner via the MySpace IM program. Other programs of this sort include the AOL Instant Messenger and MSN Live Messenger applications, which also allow visitors to chat with a profile owner. You should choose which widget or application to use based on the program that your library uses to provide chat/IM/SMS service, as well as which services your library's patrons use.

Adding Blog Widgets and Applications

MySpace's Blog feature is a great way to keep users up-to-date about library events, changes, and forthcoming additions. If your library does not already have a blog, MySpace is a great place to start. In addition to being able to write a standard blog post, the Blog tool allows you to (optionally) proclaim what your current mood is, add podcast audio files, and post what books you are reading, DVDs you're watching, etc. These additional options are perfect for libraries interested in experimenting with different techniques of outreach.

For those libraries that already have blogs up on other blogging platforms, such as WordPress or Blogger, there are often plug-ins for those tools that allow posts to appear in MySpace's Blog tool. This saves time and energy by eliminating the need to copy and paste every blog post. If you are using a different blogging platform and a cross-posting plug-in is not available, you can design your own widget using sites like WidgetBox (www.widgetbox.com) to create a blog widget to include your latest posts on your profile.

Exploring Other Widgets and Applications

The explosion of social Web sites has made it possible for libraries to reach out in a multitude of ways. **Social Reading** sites like GoodReads and LibraryThing provide widgets and applications that allow users to see what their Friends are reading as well as providing reviews for books. Including these widgets or applications on your profile can be an effective way to get users engaged with reading and book clubs.

Libraries that use Flickr or other **Photo Sharing** Web sites can use applications or widgets to include photos from those sites on the library's profile. These photo sharing services make it easier to show off the library's services and events—but don't forget to add key photos to MySpace itself!

If your library is using Twitter or another **Microblogging** application, you will find an abundance of applications and widgets available to keep your library's users in the know about the latest library news. This is also an effective way to communicate with library users who need quick assistance.

Libraries that provide services using other online services or software should check to see if HTML widgets or MySpace applications are available for those services. For example, libraries providing VOIP reference services will want to use the downloadable MySpaceIM application, which has integrated the Skype VOIP service, while those doing fundraising online can make use of "tip jar" widgets. By adding additional links to these services in your library's MySpace profile, you will be providing more points for service discovery.

Building Community on MySpace

The social nature of MySpace makes it a great place to build community around your library and its services. One rule proves consistently true: the more you use your MySpace account, the more your users will use it. A static profile implies that nothing is happening at your library and is a quick way to get your profile ignored. Use the following tools to easily keep your profile updated and to stay in touch with the library's community.

Outreach

The built-in tools within MySpace are key ways to reach out to your library's users (and potential users!). Regularly include photos, videos, and blog posts to show what is happening at the library. Change up music, movie, video game, and book preferences regularly to show what you're listening to/watching, as well as what's new in the library's collections. Libraries can use the Groups tool to coordinate committees, post online book discussions, or organize teen groups around various interests.

You can reach out to new users in a variety of ways. To start, advertise your library's MySpace profile to your regular users. Once these users add you as a Friend, many others will discover your library's page by viewing their Friends' pages. As you are friended by others, make sure to leave a comment thanking them for the add and encouraging them to ask if they need help finding anything or want to comment on the library's services. This is an informal method to help users get over library anxiety.

Advertising Events

Both public and academic librarians are recognizing the value of the library as a social place, often in correlation to the changes in bookstores, cafés, parks, and other social spaces. As such, many libraries hold public events, and MySpace is a great way to advertise those events. There are several tools that can be used to advertise events.

1. Use the Event tool (available through the "More" button on the menu) to create invitations to your event (see Figure 3.3). Users who accept invitations will have the event added to their "My Schedule" page and will be able to invite others to the event.

2. Create bulletins that advertise the event to all your Friends. Short bulletins with the major details of the event can be repeated in the weeks and last few days leading up to the event to spread the word.

3. Use your MySpace blog to give more details about the event.

4. Place classifieds (under "Community" and "Tickets & Events") to promote the event.

5. Last, encourage members of your library's groups to attend events.

Don't forget to follow up events with photos and videos of the event, as well as a blog post to say how it went. A quick bulletin thanking everyone for attending and helping will encourage future participation both from those who attended and those who did not attend.

Using MySpace for Reference and Instruction

Wherever your library's users gather, they will have questions. This is the same for your library building, the library's Web site, and your library's MySpace profile. Having easy access to reference services is helpful in each of these environments, but providing proactive help by making library instruction (and self-instruction) available is a great addition to those services. To assist in this, the library's profile should point directly to research guides, FAQs, and other resources.

▶ Figure 3.3: Creating an Event

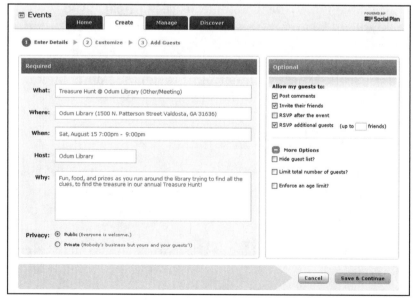

Some teachers, rather than responding to MySpace with fear and ignorance, are instead embracing the technology as a tool to engage students. Jim Brown (2006) had his students use MySpace to explore the lives of fictional characters: "By creating MySpace pages for characters in the novels we're teaching, students can think about how identities get constructed (online or otherwise) and what kinds of interests their character might have that are not explicitly mentioned in the text." Leandra Preston (2008) had her students review MySpace profiles in a women's studies course to explore trends in feminism:

> The use of "social networking activism" in my Women's Studies classes was inspired by a student discussion in a web-based introductory class about MySpace as a site of modern antifeminism. . . . I encouraged them to write about feminist and antifeminist elements of MySpace. They discovered (or recognized) a multiplicity of perspectives through their exploration. . . . Viewing MySpace profiles in a Women's Studies context motivated students to construct politically-focused, feminist MySpace profiles of their own.

In addition to MySpace, some institutions are using tools like Elgg (http://elgg.org), Ning (www.ning.com), and Moodle (http://moodle.org) to create interactive environments that help engage students with educational content. Libraries of all kinds can incorporate these social network sites to create online communities of learning and provide instruction to users.

Creating MySpace Applications

This section will show you how to create a sample MySpace application to allow your library's users to search your catalog from their homepages, their profile pages, and the application's canvas page. This is an easy way to provide additional access, marketing, and outreach for your library's users. What follows is a sample—you should change the code to search your library's catalog, not the Odum Library catalog.

Before You Begin

First, you should have a basic understanding of Web programming before you start working on developing your application. The MySpace Developer Platform and OpenSocial both use HTML and JavaScript to make applications work. If you want to learn more about these Web programming languages (or need to beef up your skills), work through some of the W3C tutorials at www.w3schools.com.

Second, MySpace has several requirements for their applications, as outlined in the Application Guidelines (http://developer.myspace.comcommunity/myspace/applicationguidelines.aspx). These guidelines are the rules by which MySpace applications will be judged before they are approved, and as such it is worth pointing out a few things for librarians to keep in mind:

▶ Applications must have unique content for each of the three types of pages (profile, home and canvas pages). This means that, in addition to a catalog search, you can provide links or embedded widgets for other library services based on the type of page and the content you want to provide.

▶ The content for each of the pages must be properly formatted to fit the pixel limitations (300 or 430 pixels wide for profile pages, 290 pixels wide for homepages, and 960 pixels wide for canvas pages).

▶ If you wish to provide a chat widget in your application, the app must be limited to those 18 years old or older. Public and school libraries will want to provide a link to their chat services rather than an embedded widget.

▶ JavaScript is limited to the canvas page only and even then can only use MySpace, Google, or Yahoo JavaScript libraries. Embedded Flash is allowed on any page.

See this book's companion wiki for downloadable sample codes for each of the three types of pages.

Writing the App

As you get ready to write your application, start by downloading the code for the MySpace version of the Odum Library Search application. This will include the HTML code for the sample Odum Library Search (this code is based on the work of Bob Trotter and Sherrida Crawford for the Odum Library homepage at www .valdosta.edu/library).

Odum Library Search App Code: MySpace Version

```
<h4>Books & Media</h4>
<a href="https://gil-odum.valdosta.edu/"
 target ="_blank">GIL@VSU Library Catalog</a>
<a href="www.valdosta.edu/library/learn/gil
 .shtml" target="_blank">
<img src="www.valdosta.edu/library/images/
 small_i.gif" alt="GIL Catalog Help" border=
 "0" align="absmiddle"></a>
<form action="www.valdosta.edu/library/
 scripts/gilsearch.php` name="multisearch" id
 ="multisearch" target="_blank">
  <input name="term" size="20" maxlength=
  "250" class="textboxstyle" type="text">
  <input name="submit" value="Go"
src="www.valdosta.edu/library/images/search_
 arrow_004.gif` alt="Search Button" align=
 "texttop" border="0" type="image"></form>
<a href="https://gil-odum.valdosta.edu/cgi-
 bin/Pwebrecon.cgi?DB=local&PAGE=bbSearch"
 target="_blank">Advanced Search</a><br>
<a href="https://giluc.usg.edu/" target="_
 blank">GIL Universal Library Catalog</a>
  ↓
```

Books & Media

GIL@VSU Library Catalog 🛈

Advanced Search
GIL Universal Library Catalog

If you do not already have a catalog search box for your library's Web site, you may need to work with your catalog vendor to perform some of the tasks in this guide. You will modify this code so that your application will search your library's catalog. You will then insert that modified code into your MySpace application for the profile, home, and canvas pages. See the sample code provided, with the parts that need to be changed bolded.

When the user searches for books or other media in the Odum Library Search application, the application will open a new window or tab and run the search using the "gilsearch.php" file on the library's Web site (see Figure 3.4). Note that *every* link in the application opens a new tab or window by using the "_blank" command. Without this command, MySpace will try to open the link within the same frame as the application, and only the first part of the results page will be visible.

Setting up the App

After you have edited the sample code to search your library's resources (and made any other customizations you like), walk through the following steps to set up the application. These steps will create a basic application, regardless of the type of application that you are writing.

1. Go to the **MySpace Developer Platform** (http://developer.myspace.com), and click on the "**Build**" link.

2. Below **Application Platform**, click on "**Create On-Site App.**"

3. Supply an Application Title, a unique e-mail address (it must be different from your MySpace account e-mail address), and a password.

4. Read through the **Developer Addendum to MySpace.com Terms of Service**, click on "I agree to the terms and conditions above," fill out the CAPTCHA, and click on "**Next.**"

5. Click on "**Skip this Step**" to bypass the XML Application screen.

6. You are now on the **Edit App Information** page. Enter a short **Application Description**.

7. Select a picture to represent your search (such as an image of your library). Resize the picture and save two copies: one at 16 × 16 pixels (for the **Small Icon**) and the other at 64 × 64 pixels (for the **Large Icon**). Now include those files.

8. Enter a **Primary Category** for your application (typically Schools & College).

9. Click on "**Save.**"

10. Click on the "**Edit App Source**" tab.

11. **Copy and paste** your customized application code into the "HTML/JavaScript Source" section of the **Canvas Surface** tab. Click on "**Save.**"

12. Repeat step 11 for the **Profile Surface** and **Home Surface** tabs.

13. Click on "**My Apps**" from the menu bar, click on your application's icon, and click on "**Add this App.**"

14. You (and your future users!) will be asked if you want the app to appear on your profile and your homepage and whether you would like to update your friends when the app changes. Check all the boxes, and click on "**Add.**"

15. Test the application.

That's it! You should now see the working application on your profile and homepage!

Making the App Available

The first step to making the application available is to publish it. You can do this by clicking on the "Publish" button next to the application on your My Apps page (http://developer.myspace .com/Apps.mvc). The application will then be reviewed by the MySpace Development Platform Team. If there are any problems with the application, you will receive an e-mail informing you what should be revised and how to resubmit your application for approval. Once the application is approved (usually within two weeks, in the author's experience), it will be made available in the Apps Gallery, where users will be able to browse and search for the application.

▶ Figure 3.4: Home View of the Odum Library Search App

All MySpace applications can be designed to allow invites. By integrating invites into your library's application, the application's users will be able to send invite messages to their MySpace Friends, encouraging them to add and use the application. Unlike spam (which is unsolicited, misleading, and automated), these invites allow users to easily share applications that they like with their Friends.

Finally, don't forget to add the application to your personal profile and your library's profile! The application should be able to be viewed, used, and added by users to their own profiles and homepages.

> As you customize your application to meet the needs of your library's users, don't forget to share what you create on the companion wiki!

Managing a MySpace Application

When users visit the application's About page, they will have the option to add the application, view the application, and post a discussion board message about the application. It is important for you to monitor the application's discussion board postings at least weekly; this way, if there are any errors, comments, or suggestions for the application, you will be able to respond to the users' needs in a timely manner. Additionally, enabling MySpace to send you an e-mail when you receive new messages will ensure that users can contact you directly (and immediately) if there are problems with the application.

Application Tips

As you get ready to create the application of your users' dreams, keep the following tips in mind. First, MySpace, like all social network sites, is primarily a social space. As such, library applications should be seen as another avenue of outreach and service and not as a replacement for the basic services libraries already provide. By creating another point for convenience and discovery of the library's resources, you will reach out to more users than before.

Second, make sure that the basic services that you are promoting work well. If you are creating a second discovery point for a catalog that returns irrelevant results, you should fix the catalog first. If you are providing another portal for users to get chat reference service when the service is not covered consistently, ensure that your users are going to get consistent, high-quality service first. This improvement of basic services ensures that those reached through social network sites will receive excellent service and will become return users.

▶ CREATE A FACEBOOK ACCOUNT

Facebook started out as a college-only social network site; it was formed at Harvard University by Mark Zukerberg in February 2004 (Yadav, 2006). In the past five years, Facebook has undergone astronomical growth—it is now ranked as the most popular social network site in the world (Alexa Internet, 2009). Although its original user base consisted of only college students, the Web site is now available to everyone (boyd and Ellison, 2007). Early in Facebook's history, librarians were using the social network site's easy communication and information sharing tools to reach out to students and classes (Landis, 2007). This interaction and exploration has continued to grow as Facebook has released new tools and applications and as enterprising librarians find new ways to reach out to their users. This section will show you how to set up and use a Facebook account, how to use that personal account to set up a profile for your library (called a "page"), and how to use and create Facebook apps.

Getting Started

Creating a personal account in Facebook is easy. A sign-up form is available from the Web site's homepage (http://facebook.com). Simply enter your full name, e-mail, a unique password, sex, and birthday. Before you click on "Sign Up," make sure that you read through the Terms of Use and the Privacy Policy.

Setting Up Your Account and Profile

At the **Getting Started** page, Facebook will ask you for three types of information to help link you up to your Friends. First it will ask you to connect your e-mail account and/or IM account to your Facebook account. Next, you will be asked to input the names of schools and businesses with which you have been associated. Last, Facebook will ask for you to identify yourself with a **Network**. Being part of a network means that you can see the profiles of other individuals in that network and that they can see your profile.

Connecting with Friends

Making connections with Friends is the central purpose of Facebook and other social network sites. I will again stress that **Friends** (with a capital F) refers to family members, friends, coworkers, acquaintances, and business contacts that you have made a profile connection with through a social network site. When you see that someone you know is also using Facebook, you can go through the act of **friending** him or her to create that connection. Adding Friends on Facebook is both easy and fun!

One fast way to connect to Friends is to link up your Facebook account with an e-mail or IM account. You can do this by choosing "Friends" from the top of the screen and selecting "Find Friends" from the drop-down menu. This will give you the option to search for Facebook contacts from:

1. your e-mail account's contact list,
2. your uploaded contact list (Outlook 2000 and later),
3. your IM account's contact list (MSN Messenger and AOL Instant Messenger only), and
4. a name or e-mail search across Facebook.

You can search for individual contacts by using the "Search for People" box or by simply typing the person's e-mail or name into the search box on the left. A listing of individuals will show up, ranked by relevance: your current Friends first, followed by exact matches, then inexact matches.

Members within your networks will have their names in blue, indicating that you can click on the name to view the profiles. You can select to "Add as Friend" if you already know the person, to "Send a Message" if you want to send a private, one-on-one message, or to "View Friends" to see who you know in common (see

Figure 3.5). Generally, you should already know or at least have spoken to a person before adding him or her as a Friend. For more information on friending etiquette, see Chapter 5: Best Practices.

Staying in Touch: Inbox, Status Updates, Pokes, Walls, Groups, and Chat

Facebook provides several different ways to communicate with your Friends. The **Inbox** allows private, one-on-one communications. You can choose to send a message to a Friend by selecting "Compose Message" from the inbox drop-down menu at the top of the screen or by searching for a Friend's profile and selecting "Send a Message."

Status Updates are a fun way to tell your Friends what you are doing. If you are working on the reference desk, cataloging puppets, or even taking a nap, a quick status update will let folks know and will also allow them to comment on what you are doing. Whenever I have to stay home sick, a quick status update will let my colleagues know I'm out for the day (and will also result in plenty of "Get well soon!" comments from my Friends!).

You can also **Poke** people in your Network. This will send a message to the user, saying that you have poked them and asking if they would like to poke you back. Poking can mean different things depending on the context of the relationship between the people, but most often it is a friendly way to say, "Hi! Remember me?"

Walls are a way to publicly exchange messages and content between profiles. Each profile has a wall, and users can write on each others' walls. Users can make comments, share links, and add content, all of which is publicly available to that user's Friends. Walls are often used for congratulations, condolences, well wishes, thanks, and other public friendly messages.

Facebook **Groups** allow users with common interests to connect with one another. Groups have been used for a variety of social and

▶ Figure 3.5: Friend Search Results

	Name:	**Cliff Landis**	Add as Friend
	Networks:	Valdosta Faculty	Send a Message
		Southern Georgia, GA	View Friends

educational purposes, from small private study groups to the "Librarians and Facebook" group with over 8,000 members! Members can use a group's page to share video, photos, discussions, wall posts, and links with each other.

Facebook also has **Chat** as part of the interface. Facebook users who have friended each other are able to chat instantaneously using Facebook's built-in instant messaging service. This is a quick way to communicate privately in real time.

As a reminder, every method of communication except for chat and inbox messages are potentially publicly visible via the news feed unless you change your privacy settings.

Showing Off: Photos, Links, Videos, Gifts, Events, and Notes

In addition to connecting with Friends, Facebook allows you to share media in a variety of ways. **Photos** can be shared by uploading files or sending mobile phone photos directly to Facebook. Users can also identify themselves and their Friends in photos by tagging the photos; this allows users to search and browse through photos for people by name.

If a Facebook user finds interesting information online, he or she can create a **Link** to that content. This link will then be shown on the user's profile. Many pages on the Web provide buttons that will help automate the posting of Facebook links.

Users can share **Videos** by uploading files, recording video directly from a Webcam, or by sending videos taken with a mobile phone straight to Facebook. Video files must be relatively small (under 2 minutes and below 100 MB).

Gifts are small icons that users can purchase to give to each other. Users can purchase gift credits with a credit card and then use those credits to give gifts to Friends; most gifts cost only 100 credits ($1 USD) and can be given privately or anonymously.

Users can use the **Events** function to advertise and invite Friends to social functions. The Events tool is especially helpful for librarians looking to market events on a small budget (see Chapter 4: Marketing), but it is also a great way to organize a get-together with friends or family!

Notes are basically blogs within Facebook. You can use the Notes tool to share personal stories and thoughts, as well as interesting things that you are working on. If you write for an external blog, you can also import that blog into Facebook's notes, saving you time and energy.

Choosing Privacy Settings

Social network users are highly aware of their privacy, and librarians are no exception. To access the Privacy Settings, select "Settings" from the Facebook Toolbar at the top of the screen. Then select "Privacy Settings." You will now have the option to choose which group of settings to edit: Profile, Search, News Feed and Wall, and Applications. This detailed degree of control over your privacy settings means that you can share as little or as much information about yourself as you like. Because privacy settings are customizable, you can limit access to particular Friends (such as close friends and family) or exclude other Friends from having access. Some librarians feel comfortable putting up their personal e-mail addresses and cell phone numbers, while many others do not. Take the time to familiarize yourself with these settings, and, remember, if you are unsure, always err on the side of caution and don't enter the information into Facebook—you can always go back and add more information about yourself later as you become more comfortable.

Your **Profile** privacy settings allow you to restrict which information is released to what groups or individuals. Again, it's up to you how much information you want to share. **Search** privacy settings allow you to restrict what information is available when people search for you. These settings will impact whether friends, family, coworkers, or other users will be able to locate your profile. This option also allows you to choose whether you want external search engines to index your profile. The **News Feed and Wall** privacy settings allow you to restrict which information about you is available on your Friends' homepages (see Figure 3.6). The **Applications** privacy settings allow you to restrict which information can be used by third-party applications. These applications often make use of information from your profile to provide extra services.

The Applications privacy menu is also where you can control privacy settings for Facebook Connect. **Facebook Connect** acts as a single sign-on service, allowing external Web sites to use Facebook

▼ Figure 3.6: Privacy Settings

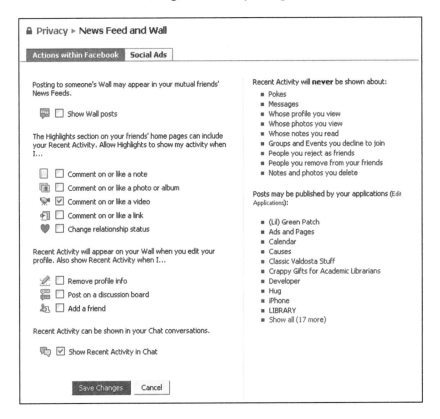

log-in and contact information to provide services and share content. This prevents users from having to re-register contact information at separate Web sites (Stone, 2008).

Knowing Your Rights (and Obligations)

By creating an account on Facebook, you are agreeing to the Terms of Service (TOS). You should read and understand the entire TOS; however, several clauses within the TOS are of particular interest to libraries and librarians and should be noted. First, you should know that by posting anything to Facebook, you are granting Facebook the right to distribute and keep a copy of that content, even if you delete your account. It should also go without saying that you must have the right or permission to post something on Facebook (www.facebook.com/terms.php, "Licenses").

Librarians should do the same thing that we advise our users to do: think before you upload. This should not strike fear into the hearts of librarians or users but, instead, be understood as part of using Facebook and gaining all the benefits of a social network.

Second, it should be noted that your Facebook account, page, or app can be removed at any time without notice (www.facebook .com/terms.php, "Termination and Changes to the Facebook Service"). As the development of Facebook changes over time, various parts of the service may be offered or withdrawn without notice. This caused some problems in the past, when librarians created profiles for their libraries (which was against the TOS), and these profiles were later deleted without advanced notice by Facebook (Drew, 2006). More than a year later, Facebook pages were offered as a way for users to create Facebook content for institutions and organizations (Ostrow, 2007). This should serve as a warning to always read the TOS carefully and always save your content somewhere else, and then use Facebook to share it.

Last, note that the TOS can change at any time. You should check back regularly to make sure that the rules have not changed drastically. In addition to the regular TOS, there are additional terms regarding privacy (www.facebook.com/policy.php), Facebook pages (www.facebook.com/terms_pages.php), and Facebook apps (http://developers.facebook.com/user_terms.php). Each of these should also be read and understood.

Facebook Pages

Because Facebook does not allow nonhumans to have profiles (you can't create a profile for your library, for example), pages were created to allow users to interact around various nonhuman entities. These pages are not a replacement for the library's Web site but instead an added point of discovery and entry to using the library's resources. Facebook pages make it possible for organizations, objects, concepts, and events to have representation in Facebook. Here are a few examples:

> ▶ A library, such as Odum Library (www.facebook.com/pages/ Valdosta-GA/Odum-Library/6873663367)

- ▶ A blog, such as The Free Range Librarian (www.facebook .com/pages/Free-Range-Librarian/14363510777)
- ▶ A thing, such as Caffeine (www.facebook.com/pages/ Caffeine/42540642867)
- ▶ A concept, such as Happiness (www.facebook.com/pages/ Happiness/14299131635)
- ▶ A public figure, such as Chuck Norris (www.facebook.com/ pages/Chuck-Norris/32849897028)

Facebook pages also have added benefits that make them better for organizations such as libraries. Users can become "Fans" of a Facebook page, thereby indicating their interest in the page's topic. Fans can then receive informative updates as the page is up-dated or as special notices are posted by the page's administrators. Pages can have multiple administrators, which makes managing a library's page easy. Because individual librarians can sign in with their own profile to edit the library's page, they need to keep track of less log-in information.

Creating a Page

Creating a page for your library is simple:

1. Navigate your browser to www.facebook.com/pages/create .php.
2. From the Category section, choose the "Local" option and select "**Library/Public Building**."
3. Fill in the words from the security test and select "Create Page."

That's it! You can now add information about your library (such as its address, hours of operation, and where users can find a parking space), as well as a branding picture to help visually identify the li-brary. Once you are done making the initial edits, remember to "Publish" your page to make it viewable to the public.

Facebook pages come preloaded with a variety of applications. Most of these will be the same as those on your Facebook profile, such as a wall, photos, videos, links, notes, etc. In addition, like groups, pages come with events and discussion boards, which will allow your users to interact with each other and your staff. You can also add additional applications to your page, such as those you create yourself in the next section!

Using the Page Tools

Once your page has been published and users begin to visit it, Facebook will automatically gather and analyze data about your page's visitors and Fans. The **Insights** tool allows you to see a variety of information about your page in graph format, including the number of page views, new Fans, wall posts, reviews, photo views, etc. (see Figure 3.7). This information can be very helpful when gathering measurement data for metrics and can also be used to measure the effectiveness of an advertising campaign on Facebook (see Chapter 6, "Measures of Success").

As your library's page gathers Fans, you can send **Updates** to those Fans. Updates are a method of push marketing where you can send messages to anyone who has become a Fan of your li-

▶ Figure 3.7: Insights

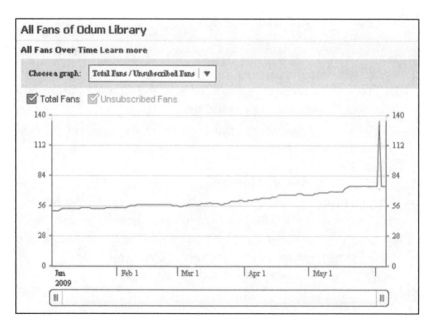

brary's page. These messages can include information such as events, contests, changes in hours, or new page content. Users will get these messages in their Inbox on the Updates tab. As with all forms of push marketing, be careful not to overload your Fans with too many updates. Doing so can reduce the effectiveness of important updates and possibly cost you some Fans should they become annoyed with the barrage of information.

Pages can also add other pages as **Favorites** (similar to how users can Friend each other). This tool allows you to draw connections between various groups and organizations that are represented with Facebook pages. For example, your library could add the American Library Association Student Chapters (www.facebook .com/pages/American-Library-Association-Student-Chapters/359137 08659) or Reading (www.facebook.com/pages/Jordan/Reading/ 26958092071) as favorites. This method of association is an easy way to cross-market related organizations. Public libraries can add other libraries in the system as favorites, while academic libraries can add their college or university as a favorite page.

Getting Fans

Your library's page will get new Fans from a variety of places because of Facebook's interconnected social nature. Once an individual becomes a Fan of your library, it is likely that the user's Friends will see this on their news feeds. This visibility makes it likely that other users will become Fans of your page at the same time. Over time, you will notice spikes where several people will become Fans all at once as your library's page spreads through social circles.

As your Friends slowly spread the word, your library's page will grow with time. This organic social growth can also be augmented by regularly updating content, advertising, and using Facebook to organize events, discussions, and the dissemination of media like photos and videos. See Chapter 4 (Marketing) and Chapter 5 (Best Practices) for more on these topics.

Facebook Applications

Librarians' first reaction to a new technology is usually to make their traditional services available in a new format. As such, when Facebook released the Developer Platform to allow users to create applications in May 2007, librarians were quick to make services such as chat reference, catalog searches, and library blogs available in this new medium. As of November 2009, a search for "library catalog search" in Facebook revealed over 36 applications (www.facebook.com/s.php?q=library+catalog+search). This section will introduce you to some of the applications that are available for extending the library's services.

Finding, Installing, and Managing Applications

Facebook applications can be found by doing a Facebook search for your topic or the name of the application. You can install the application on your profile by clicking on "Go to Application." If the application is available to be added to pages, you can click on "Add to Page" to do so. You will be asked whether you want to "Allow Access" to the application—many applications harvest a user's information to provide service, such as connecting to an external Web site or accessing a user's Friends list. If you are uncomfortable with the application having access, you can always adjust the application's privacy settings, or you can uninstall the application.

You can navigate to the "Application Settings" menu from the main "Settings" menu if you would like to adjust a particular application. In most cases, you can adjust notification frequency (whether the application can post messages to your wall), privacy and box settings, bookmark settings (to make the application more easily available to you), and any additional permissions (such as whether the application can e-mail you). By managing these settings right after adding an application, you gain greater control over the information that you provide and receive through Facebook.

Adding Chat Reference Apps

Many libraries have expanded into digital reference service by providing chat or instant messaging service. Libraries use a variety of programs to provide chat service, including AOL Instant Messenger, Yahoo Messenger, Windows Live Messenger, Jabber, and Google Talk. Some libraries also use chat aggregators to collect these individual chat services into a single place. Examples of these aggregators include Pidgin, Adium, Trillian, Meebo, and Fire. Also, some libraries use embedded chat apps that allow users to ask questions via chat without downloading any software or having to create accounts. This allows users to be anonymous and decreases the work that they have to do to get library help. Examples of these Web-based apps include LibraryH3lp, MeeboMe, AIM Wimzi, Plugoo, and a variety of home-grown services.

Facebook, as a social environment, is a perfect place to distribute chat reference service. In some cases, applications are already available for Facebook users. Services such as MeeboMe (www.facebook.com/apps/application.php?&id=2354779593) and AIM Wimzi (www.facebook.com/apps/application.php?id=2399464987) can be added to librarian profiles as a way for users to ask for help.

In addition to these applications, Facebook also has its own chat service available to users. As librarians add library users to their Friends list, they should not be surprised if they get the occasional question or comment about the library from Facebook chat.

Adding Blog Applications

Many libraries today write blogs as a way to inform users about new resources, library and community events, book reviews, and other topics. Integrating your library's blog into its Facebook page (or writing one within Facebook) is a great way to spread the word about what your library is doing. Applications are available for most major blog publishing software, including WordPress, LiveJournal, Movable Type, Blogger, Twitter, FriendFeed, and TypePad.

There are two types of blog applications: pull and push. Pull applications will pull blog posts from your external blog into Facebook; also, the notes application will perform this function for any RSS feed. Push applications will allow you to write a post within Facebook and have it appear on an external blog. Both types of applications can be found by performing a quick Facebook search for your blogging software of choice.

Adding Other Kinds of Applications

Libraries have taken advantage of the boom in social software to provide their services in new and innovative ways. Rather than providing traditional Web guides, many libraries have transitioned to **Social Bookmarking**. Services such as Delicious, Stumble Upon, Gnolia, and reddit all have Facebook applications that will import bookmarked Web pages for Friends or Fans to see.

Many information providers are starting to recognize the power of having **Search Interfaces** available through social networks. As such, you can now add JSTOR, Google News, WorldCat, and other search applications to your profile or your library's page. These applications provide a great way for users to discover what resources their library has available.

If your library provides user services through other software or online services, check to see if a Facebook application is available. For example, libraries providing VOIP reference using Skype, or organizing subject guides with LibGuides, will likely want to add those Facebook applications to their library's page. Providing this additional exposure to the library's services will likely attract new users for those services.

Building Community on Facebook

Social network sites like Facebook allow users to create community in a way that has never been seen before. Librarians can now connect with users on a personal, human level, reducing library anxiety and increasing interest and access to the library. All of this is possible through social network sites, yet one rule is consistently visible: the more you keep your library's page active, the more your library's users will interact with it. A static Facebook page implies that there is little or no interest in reaching out to users.

Outreach

Keeping your library's Facebook page (and your personal profile) active is a sure way to reach out to users. Consistent updates with photos, links, videos, wall posts, and notes will keep your site interesting and will also show users all the cool and innovative things that the library is doing.

Outreach to your library's regular users is the first start to reaching a larger audience. These people will be your library's cheerleaders, extolling the wonders of your library and the helpfulness of your library's workers. Some of these users' Friends will soon add your library's page to stay up-to-date with all the latest developments. In a personal e-mail, Laura Kohl describes this face-to-face marketing of her library's Facebook page to students who are already "living" on Facebook:

> At The Douglas & Judith Krupp Library at Bryant University we consider our various social network sites to be quite successful. Whenever we tell students to become a fan of our Facebook page, we sometimes get a giggle, yet, they do it. We only recently started a Twitter presence, yet students are following. And of course the ability to use the sites for instructional resources is huge. We have a librarian who is experimenting with using a Facebook page to share subject specific resources for a Legal Studies class. The opportunities are endless and the students are already living there and familiar, what's not to like. (Kohl, personal communication, October 15, 2009)

You can also reach out to new users by mentioning your library's Facebook page (and your own account) in conversation. During library instruction sessions, I will often tell students that they can reach me via phone, e-mail, chat, Facebook or MySpace—whatever service they prefer. Inevitably, I return to my office to find that at least one of the students from the session has friended me. This serves as a convenient bookmark for these students; if they ever need to find me again, all they have to do is type "library" or "librarian" into their search box, and I will pop up in their Friends list.

Marketing with Events and Facebook Advertisements

Beyond marketing services through everyday activity, many libraries spread their outreach efforts by coordinating events through Facebook, as well as purchasing ads on Facebook. Most libraries regularly host events to reach out to users and to encourage the use of the library's collection and services. The Events tool allows users to RSVP to events, as well as to spread the word about those events. Guests can invite other guests, and Facebook will automatically promote events to users whose Friends have said that they will attend.

If you are willing to spend money to attract a larger audience, you can reach out to users with Facebook advertisements. Simply log in to Facebook and click on the "Advertisements" link at the bottom of the screen. You can create a customized ad that will reach a specific target audience; this will allow you to reach out to only those users in your network, as well as users of a specific demographic and those with particular interests. Additionally, you can choose a budget, a date range for deployment, and a pricing method, all of which further allow you to target for specific campaigns or events. Advertisements also come with analytics, so you can see which advertisements are reaching which types of users. This will allow you to further hone your advertising skills for future events or service promotions.

Community-Building with Groups and Applications

The Groups tool is an effective way to reach out to subsets of your library's users. You will often find that study groups, student organizations, and community gatherings of users will organize themselves via Facebook. A quick search for your library's name will show these organizations and allow you to reach out on behalf of your library to provide any assistance that they may need. Some librarians may fear that this would appear as intruding on their social space online, but, instead, by contacting the group's leaders, the library can reach out to the community, further strengthening needed ties.

Groups are also used by Facebook users for humor and identity performance. In fact, a quick search for your library's name may reveal that users have already created groups that involve your library. For example, my own library, Odum Library, is mentioned in several humorous groups, such as "4th Floor Odum Library Bathroom Users" (where the bathroom is supposedly cleaner!), and "Odum Library Is Only Good for One Thing and That Thing Is Facebook!!" Because these groups are open, I enjoy occasionally popping in to see what students are saying, but I don't join or participate; I am sensitive to the fact that my presence as a library faculty member would spoil the fun of the group, even though there is no attempt to make the group private. For more tips on how to interact with users in these situations, see Chapter 5: Best Practices.

Applications are another fun, community-building tool. Despite the fact that many libraries have created apps to search their resources, the most popular "library" application on Facebook is "Library Gifts," a fun social application that allows users to give each other library-themed gifts. Examples of these gifts include "Libraries are . . . For all generations of info seekers!" and "Libraries Are . . . Full of helpful information professionals!" (www.facebook.com/apps/application.php?id=15520516777). Other applications allow you to show off your school spirit, gather support for social and political causes, and simply send goodwill to fellow Facebook users. Each of these applications (and many more) allows users to interact at the grassroots social level. This is yet another illustration of the power behind social network sites—the ability to connect individuals with common interests, regardless of the distance that separates them.

Using Facebook for Instruction

Because of its initial popularity with college students, many higher education faculty have tried using Facebook as a learning management tool. This can be successful, because many students are comfortable with Facebook and are often logged into the tool anyway. However, because Facebook is primarily a social tool, it can sometimes blur the lines between the social and academic/professional realms, which can have mixed results.

Dr. Patrick Biddix explains his success having his students discuss theories of student development using Facebook:

> Students began posting as soon as they were friended into the group, and would periodically post quick thoughts throughout the day as classmates posted. In this way, students actually posted more often than on a normal forum in Blackboard. When I asked the students, they said it was because they were

already logged into Facebook and it was just "easier" than
having to remember to log into Blackboard, find the post,
read to catch-up and then post their own thought. The
Facebook discussions seemed alive—more like an actual conversation between several people than static posts on a board.
(Biddix, personal communication, February 18, 2009)

However, Dr. Biddix noticed that this did not work for all topics.
When discussions of race and African-American development theory were raised on the class's private Facebook discussion boards,
students were more reluctant to post online than they were to discuss the topics in class. When asked why, students responded, "You
can gauge what the others think about your posts, or the flow of
the conversation and adjust your view as you need. Online, you
can't do this. Sure, you can retract a post, but it is more difficult to
gauge mood." Dr. Biddix used this information to inform the
course's development. "I believe I could tie in the in-class discussions on sensitive or controversial topics back to online reticence,
but I believe when working with issues that are sensitive to students
(e.g., otherness, oppression, isms), it is equally important to create
an environment that is as safe and comfortable as possible to facili-
tate meaningful learning."

This is an excellent example of the value of Facebook for course
deployment, but it also shows some of the limitations of online
classes (and online communication) in general. It is interesting,
however, that students were aware that they could be misunder-
stood if they did not carefully craft their words on a sensitive topic.
Despite students' wariness about posting on sensitive topics online, the class successfully had students posting more often and
in a more engaged way than they would have through the university's course management software. Librarians who are interested in teaching online, or providing in-class support for another
teacher's course, should consider Facebook as a method of
instruction. There are several Facebook groups devoted to this
topic, including Classroom Instruction in Facebook (www
.facebook.com/group.php?gid=2416166855) and Blended Learning and Instruction (www.facebook.com/group.php?gid=
7929669410).

Creating Facebook Applications

This section will walk you through the steps of developing a sample library catalog search application. This application will allow Facebook users to search your library's Web-based catalog from within Facebook—an excellent addition to your library's page! Users will also be able to add this search box to their own profiles and pages, allowing them to further market your library's services. What follows is a sample—you should change the code in the application to search your library's catalog, not the Odum Library catalog.

Before You Begin

First, you should have a basic understanding of Web programming. This includes skills in HTML, CSS, and PHP. Facebook uses FBML (Facebook Markup Language, its own proprietary HTML-derived language) for deploying applications. If you are interested in learning these skills before you begin (or if you need a refresher), check out the tutorials available from the W3C Web site (www.w3schools.com).

Second, you will need server space. There are services out there that will give limited free hosting for social network applications, such as Joyent (www.joyent.com). However, many libraries already have the small space necessary to host a catalog search application.

Third, you will need the appropriate permission to play around on the server. If you are not the "tech" person at your library, now is the time to make friends with him or her. You will need to have access to upload, download, and change files on the server. You should also make the technology folks at your library aware that, depending on the application's success, it may require extra system resources (bandwidth, etc.).

Writing the App

Start by downloading and looking at the code for the Odum Library Search application from this book's companion wiki. This includes the five files that you will need to modify and upload to your server space. (This code is based on the work of David Ward at UIUC; check out www.facebook.com/apps/application.php?id= 2414276217. All thanks are due to David for releasing the original code and making it possible for other librarians to follow his example.) The sample files given use PHP 5, so if your server uses a different version of PHP, you may need to alter the files further.

Open the info.php file, and edit the code to include a form to search your library's catalog. Often this code can be taken directly

---

Odum Library Search App Code: Facebook Version

```
<h3>Books & Media</h3>
```
Search the <a href="https://gil-odum.valdosta.edu/">GIL@ VSU Library Catalog</a>
```
<a href="http://www.valdosta.edu/library/
learn/gil.shtml">
<img src="http://www.valdosta.edu/library/
images/small_i.gif" alt="GIL Catalog Help"
border="0" align="absmiddle"></a>
<form action="http://www.valdosta.edu/
library/scripts/gilsearch.php" name=
"multisearch" id="multisearch">
  <input name="term" size="20" maxlength=
  "250" class="textboxstyle" type="text">
  <input name="submit" value="Go" src=
  "http://www.valdosta.edu/library/ images
  /search_arrow_004.gif" alt="Search Button"
  align="texttop" border="0" type="image"></
  form>
<a href="https://gil-odum.valdosta.edu/
cgi-bin/Pwebrecon.cgi?DB=local&amp;PAGE=bbSe
arch">Advanced Search</a>
  <a href="https://giluc.usg.edu/">GIL
  Universal Library Catalog</a>
↓
```

Books & Media
Search the GIL@VSU Library Catalog ⓘ

Advanced Search GIL Universal Library Catalog

---

from your library's homepage. (The code for the Odum Library Search was taken directly from code written by Bob Trotter and Sherrida Crawford for the Odum Library homepage at www .valdosta.edu/library.) If you don't have a catalog search box on your library's Web site, you may need to work with your catalog vendor to develop one.

So when a Facebook user searches for a book in the Odum Library Search application, the application will use the "gilsearch .php" script on the library's Web site to search the library's catalog (see Figure 3.8).

▶ Figure 3.8: Odum Library Search Application on Facebook

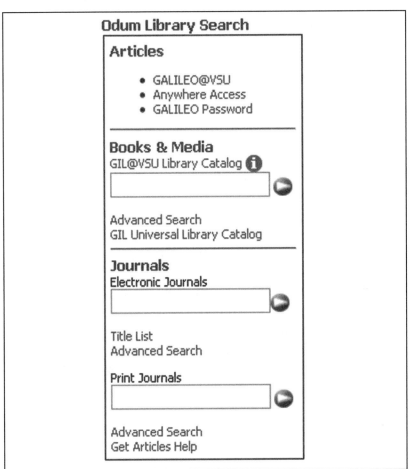

Setting up the App

Once you have customized the info.php file to search your library's catalog, these are the steps to take, in order, to set up the application. These are generally the steps that should be taken, regardless of the type of application:

1. Add the **Facebook Developer Application** to your Facebook account (www.facebook.com/developers/).

2. Click on the "**Set Up New Application**" button.

3. Type in the **Application Name**. For this example, we'll call our application *Test Library Search.*

4. Read through the Facebook Platform Terms of Service (http://developers.facebook.com/terms.php), and then click on "**Agree and Save Changes.**"

5. This will take you to the **Edit Settings** page, where you can edit the settings for your application. You will see that the application has been issued an Application ID, an API Key, and a Secret. Save all three of these numbers in a secure place.

6. Under "Basic Information," enter the **Callback URL**. This is the *directory* on your servers where the application will live. Next, enter in a short **Description** of the application. Then you will upload a photo that will be automatically resized to serve as the **Icon** and the **Logo** (I recommend using a relatively square image and using the same image for both the icon and logo). Click on "**Save Changes.**"

7. On the left menu, select "**Authentication.**" Allow the application to be added by both **Users** and **Facebook Pages**.

8. On the left menu, select "**Canvas.**" Now you will create your **Canvas URL**. This is the page that serves as your application's location on Facebook, so you will want the URL to be short and descriptive. We will call our application *Test-Library-Search.*

9. Go to the files that you downloaded, open the **appinclude .php** file, and replace the **$appapikey** and **$appsecret** lines with your application's API Key and Secret, respectively.

Then replace the **$url** line with the location of the info .php file on your server. Replace the **$appcallbackurl** with the *directory* on the server in which your files will be located.

10. Upload the files to your server.

11. Test the app.

That's all there is to it! At this point, you should have a working catalog search application!

Making the App Available

Although it is relatively quick and easy to get an application up and running, it takes a little more time to make it truly integrated into the Facebook experience. Users can access applications in a variety of ways, so it pays to invest the extra time necessary to make sure that your application is fully accessible from anywhere in Facebook.

First, click on "**Edit About Page**" to add more information about your application. Then you should edit the "Application Information" to include a description of the application, the application's category (Education), and information about yourself as the individual developer. All this information will make the application more searchable.

After you have filled in all the necessary information, get five of your Friends to add the application. This, along with having the above information filled out, will make it possible to submit your application to the **Facebook Application Directory**. This directory allows users to search or browse for your application. You can submit your application by going to the developers application, choosing "My Applications," and then clicking on the "Submit It" link.

Next, click the "Edit Application" link and select "**User Profiles.**" These options allow users and pages to add your application to their profiles, allowing quicker access to the application. The **Profile Tab** options will allow users to have a tab dedicated to your application on their profile. Under "Profile Tab," choose a tab name (Test Library Search), and a tab URL (the URL for the actual search box we created: info.php). The **Profile Box** option allows users to have the search application appear on the user's main profile page. Choose whether your application will be narrow (184 pixels wide) or wide (380 pixels wide).

Last, don't forget to add the application to your profile and pages! The application should now be complete and working, viewable to your library's users, and addable to user profiles and pages in a variety of ways. As you will see when you navigate the application menus, there are many other options available to further enhance your application.

> Feel free to develop your application beyond the extent in this guide, and remember to share your findings on the companion wiki!

Managing a Facebook Application

Each Facebook application has an About Page that has many of the same features as your library's page. Users can use the About Page to write reviews of the application, post messages on the wall, see which of their Friends also have added the app, or use the discussion board to ask questions and get help. You should monitor the About Page at least weekly to ensure that any problems or discussions can receive timely responses. Additionally, you should enable Facebook to send you e-mails when you receive direct messages to ensure that any immediate problems can be communicated quickly.

Application Tips

Before you get started developing an application, here are a few tips to keep in mind. First, it should again be pointed out that social network sites are primarily social spaces. Therefore, librarians should not think of Facebook applications as a solution to a problem but rather see them as another discovery point, allowing users to discover the path to the library's services.

Second, your basic service should work before you develop an application to expand its exposure. If your catalog's basic search returns irrelevant results, you should work on fixing that problem before you develop an application. If many of your chat users leave the chat page because the librarians aren't answering their questions fast enough, the last thing you need to do is spread that lack of service to another medium. By first focusing on improving our basic services, we are then able to provide high-quality service to more users through social network sites.

►4

MARKETING

- ► **Develop a Marketing Plan**
- ► **Update Your Library's Brand Identity**
- ► **Combine Push and Pull Marketing**
- ► **Create a Social Marketing Campaign**

One of the biggest benefits of having a library presence on a social network site is the ability to reach a wide audience with very little expense. However, the use of social network sites for marketing should be tied into the library's overall marketing plan. This chapter will explain the basics of effectively developing a marketing plan that includes social network sites and developing effective cross-platform brands. You will also learn about crafting marketing campaigns and using both push and pull marketing to attract users.

► DEVELOP A MARKETING PLAN

Despite the immense power of social network sites as marketing tools, they cannot do the job alone. Each library should develop a marketing plan for social network sites that integrates with the library's overall strategic plan. Strategic planning helps both library workers and library users understand the overall vision, mission, and values that drive the library forward. This planning process should be ongoing and allow all stakeholders to have the opportunity to comment; some of the best ideas for library marketing and improvements come from users and frontline staff.

Your marketing plan, as part of the larger strategic plan, should include using the library's social network site as both a tool and a product. The library's profile will serve as a point of outreach for social network site users, and it will also be a drawing point for technologically connected users who use social network sites heavily. The following steps will help you craft an effective marketing plan.

Know Your User

Part of the mission of libraries is to help everyone find the information that they need, so it can be tempting to try to reach *every potential user* by spreading general marketing materials as far as possible. However, it is much more effective to focus on small groups of users, catering your marketing efforts to target those groups. This is where social network sites are particularly effective. A few years ago, social network sites were mostly populated by teenagers and young adults, but that is swiftly changing (comScore, 2006). In March 2009, Facebook's fastest-growing population was women over 55, with users 35–44 being the largest group of new users (Smith, 2009). Still, much of the population found on these sites is tech-savvy early adopters; knowing this ahead of time can help you craft your outreach.

Much of the information gathered during planning can be used to further enhance your marketing plan (see Chapter 2, "Planning"). Additionally, you can use census and other government data, paper and telephone surveys, and focus groups to understand the populations that you serve. Most importantly, remember to ask your library's users what they want from the library—librarians can brainstorm about what users want as much as they like, but they will naturally skew the results based on their own biases. There is no substitute for directly asking a user what he or she needs.

Because not all users are on social network sites, it pays to know where your users get their information and what information resources they are most interested in. In his presentation *Friending Libraries: Why Libraries Can Become Nodes in People's Social Networks*, Lee Rainey (2009) discusses the different types of users and what services they seek that the library can offer. Groups like the Tech

Indifferent (10 percent of the population), Information Encumbered (10 percent of the population), and Drifting Surfers (14 percent of the population) might be more likely to encounter marketing efforts in traditional media (direct mail, radio, TV, etc.) or more traditional forms of Internet marketing (such as e-mail or banner advertisements) (Rainey, 2009).

Know Your Library

Being able to appropriately market your services requires that you understand the demand for those services. Now that your user groups are identified, you can identify or develop programs and services that meet those groups' needs. In many cases, you may already have services that meet the needs of your community, but the community may not know about those services. For example, look at this comment from an online message board (with original spelling intact):

> was just thinking. my sister does -alot- of reading, and spends like $1000 a year on just books alone. most of them she reads once then never looks at again. is there any kind of like . . . video rental store but for books? would make things alot cheaper, plus once one person had read one the next person can get enjoyment from it etc. ("book rental service?", 2008)

This points to a severe lack of marketing on the part of libraries, but, more interestingly, these book rental services actually exist.

BookSwim (http://bookswim.com) and BookRenter (www.bookrenter.com) will directly mail books to users for a price. These services have arisen because libraries do not provide direct home mailing for items, nor do most libraries carry the latest editions of expensive textbooks. By identifying users' needs, commercial entities have been able to meet users' needs that libraries have refused to do, even though these services could have been revenue-generating ventures for libraries. However, there are many services that have been developed in recent years due to demand from users (such as manga and anime collections or downloadable audiobooks). By knowing your users' needs, you can design services to meet those needs, further adding value to your library.

Again, I should emphasize that your library's services should be in good working order before you attempt to market them. Christine Koontz points out how library users' expectations are changing as a result of the excellent experiences they receive at the hands of commercial information providers (as summarized in Siess, 2003: 1–2):

> [L]ibrary users are now also customers who demand, choose and select among information products. . . . They expect the information we deliver to be accurate, timely, and of value. They expect friendly employees, an attractive and easy-to-use facility, a wide and well-reasoned selection of resources, and a host of other wide-ranging and ever-changing services and products.

Because the bar has been raised, libraries need to meet the raised expectations of users or risk losing them. By creating Google Alerts or Twitter Alerts using your library's name, you can see when users are commenting on your library's resources and services, as well as be able to respond to the changing needs of your users.

▶ UPDATE YOUR LIBRARY'S BRAND IDENTITY

The library as an institution already has a brand: books. In most users' minds, that is all a library is. In examining OCLC's 2005 report, *Perceptions of Libraries and Information Resources,* Roy Tennant (2006) points out that users still consider the library's brand to be books and books alone:

> We have our work cut out for us. Our support is in most cases directly connected to how we are perceived by our users—as it should be. If we are not there for them in ways they expect, or if we can't expand their expectations to meet our new capabilities, then we will find ourselves no more than the repositories of books many people apparently believe us to be.

So, the task of marketing and changing the library's brand is more than "one more thing to do"; it is directly tied to our funding and future existence. Changing this image of the library as a book repository will take the effort of all librarians everywhere. This change requires librarians to reach out directly to users and also to revise the image of their libraries. This can be done in large part by developing a brand—a symbol (visual, auditory, textual, etc.) that identifies one organization or product and separates it from others.

Branding is more than selecting a color palate or some of your library's best features and presenting them. As Elisabeth Doucett (2009: 11–12) explains, brands have power because they tell stories:

> A library might tell its patrons that it provides them with a connection to their community. Emotional branding is generally seen as more powerful than attribute branding because emotions themselves are so powerful. If you can develop a brand that taps into the emotional perspective of your potential users, then odds are that you have developed a powerful story about your library in the minds of those individuals.

Libraries are inherently part of a community, whether it's a local geographic community for public libraries, an educational community for school and university libraries, or a community of practice for special libraries. By identifying the relationship between the library and the community, and then drawing upon the values of the community, the library's brand can send an emotional message.

This usage of emotional, community-based brands can be seen in several libraries' MySpace profiles. The eVolver profile of the Denver Public Library Teens (www.myspace.com/denver_evolver) has a color and graphic scheme that is similar to (but funkier than!) the main Denver Public Library's Web page (http://denverlibrary.org). Additionally, the eVolver profile includes both social and academic resources; teens can get help from librarians and search the catalog, but they can also follow the teen program's Twitter account and view the latest student-made book review video (see Figure 4.1).

Another example is The Loft (www.myspace.com/libraryloft), the branded MySpace profile for the ImaginOn teen library of

▶ Figure 4.1: eVolver MySpace Profile

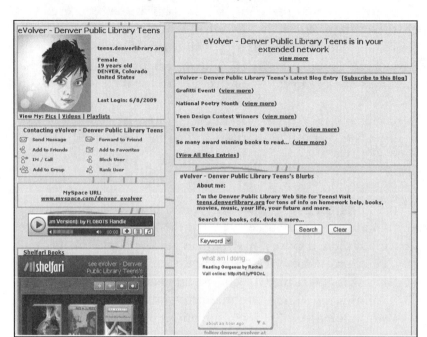

Charlotte & Mecklenburg County, North Carolina (www.imaginon .org). The library's profile provides a catalog search and an instant messenger box to ask librarians for help. However, more notably, the profile includes flyers for each of the events that the library hosts. Additionally, the profile includes a calendar of events, cover art for popular teen fiction, and pictures from past events. Because MySpace allows you to edit your profile's look and feel, it is easy to create a visual brand identity.

In Facebook, libraries developing brand identity have to do so within the limitations of Facebook's pages; this can often lead to bland, text-only pages. However, some libraries have become quite adept at working within Facebook's limitations to include photos, video, and interesting status updates to develop a library brand. The Topeka & Shawnee County Public Library's Facebook page (www.facebook.com/pages/Topeka-KS/Topeka-Shawnee-County -Public-Library/5530982975) includes images with many of the events advertised, uses a Facebook application to make its YouTube videos available on the page, and provides a space for discussions. For my own institution, Valdosta State University's Odum Library (www.facebook.com/pages/Valdosta-GA/Odum-Library/ 6873663367), we use images of users for the library's profile picture rather than an image of the library building. Posts to the library's blog are automatically imported into the page's wall, and the blog posts are mostly photos around the library or interesting additions to the collection (rather than bland informational updates). Photos available on the page include the building but also pictures of students from past events, librarians, and even pictures of the otters that swim in the creek outside the library! Despite being an academic library, we feel it is important to stress the approachability of the library, as well as the library's central place in the university community. By recognizing that building a brand image is less about what you say and more about how you say it, libraries are able to have success in branding themselves in Facebook despite its visual constraints.

▶ COMBINE PUSH AND PULL MARKETING

Traditional "push" marketing consists of creating a brand to push products and services out to the user. By reaching a wide audience, the message is received by those few individuals who have an interest in that product or service. This form of marketing is designed for products that are already in place or are in the final development stages. Libraries are familiar with this form of marketing, as they will often adopt a new software or service, implement it, and then market it hoping that users will make use of it. Push marketing is effective when you know that there is a steady demand for products and services (bestsellers, WiFi Internet access, etc.), but might be less effective for experimental products and services.

"Pull" marketing, on the other hand, is based on the needs of individual users. Products and services are only supplied as users request them, thereby limiting the need for stocking inventory but increasing the wait time of users. Libraries are familiar with this system of marketing and supply too—we use it for interlibrary loan. Users have access to records for more items than the library houses, with the understanding that those items can be supplied after a short wait.

Pull marketing has become more sophisticated in our information economy as companies begin to add value to their services by supplying information as well as products. The Pampers brand diapers Web site (www.pampers.com) is a perfect example. Expectant mothers can register at the Web site for free to get information about parenting and to track the progress of their child, from fetus to toddler. According to brand manager Guillaume Tardy (Marketing Week, 2006), links to Pampers products are available but unobtrusive, which has made the site successful:

> But the price of this success is abstinence—no pushing the product. "We are giving information that goes beyond traditional brand boundaries," says Tardy, and user attitudes are quite clear. "Anything that can help them is welcome, so long as it is not intrusive. But as soon as it gets too promotional or brand-centric, they immediately switch off."

Because libraries aren't trying to sell anything, we actually have an advantage over the competition. Yet, we can use the same tactics to reach out to customers and lead them to other authoritative information resources that they might need.

Libraries' social network site profiles combine the best of both push and pull marketing. The profile itself gives users a gateway to discovery of the library's resources. General messages are broadcast in the form of events, flyers, status updates, photos, videos, etc. If these messages are broadcast in a user-centric way, the user will be invited to explore further. Therefore, it is also important that the profile give the user direct access to a quick, responsive, friendly library worker. It is this access that reaches out to users on individual, personal, and social levels. Users can then get an information retrieval experience that is catered to their needs and desires.

▶ CREATE A SOCIAL MARKETING CAMPAIGN

Libraries are eternally facing tight budgets, so social network sites can often seem like a marketing pot of gold. With absolutely no investment of money, you can see a large return in library usage. However, this image is an illusion, because social network sites require regular planning, content creation, and updating, all of which is an investment of both time and energy. Follow these tips to help ensure that your time and energy are spent wisely!

Keep it user-centric. Your library, and by extension your library's social network site profile, should reflect the needs of the user, not the librarian or library brand. Reach out to your users and discover what they need, and make that information readily available via the library's profile. Provide ample information to help your users get in touch with a librarian to meet their other information needs.

Offer something of value. Many users may not know of all the services that your library offers or even that most of those services are free! Focus on what you can provide your users that they can't get from commercial booksellers, online search engines, or coffee shops. Reflect this in your library's profile.

Give them an experience. Humans are sensual creatures. As we experience each moment, we want to see, feel, hear, taste, and touch our environment. Your social network site profile should include images, video, audio, interactive demonstrations, and other resources that will give them a rich user experience. Tie this in with imagery and text describing your library, inviting them to get a similarly rich experience in person.

Make it interactive. Showcase user-created content, and invite users to produce similar content. Many social network site users are adept at creating and uploading content and will enjoy showing off their skills. Contests to create promotional materials for the library are a great way to do all of these, while getting more marketing materials!

Make it memorable. If something is funny, interesting, innovative, or cool, it will spread quickly through the Internet. The most successful content has all four of these characteristics. The power of the social Web is that users share—when one user loves your content, he or she will share it with friends, who will then share it with their friends, and so on; this is called viral marketing. By taking the extra time to develop interesting content from library workers or library users (or even better—both!), you will be able to draw attention to the library with less long-term effort.

Make it shareable. This is the other component to viral marketing. Social network sites enable the quick spreading of information, so make sure that your marketing materials are ready to spread across the Internet. Integrate your profile with any applicable outside tools (photo-sharing sites, blogs, video-sharing sites, microblogging tools, social bookmarking sites, wikis, etc.), so that information can be broadcast by users quickly and easily. Ensure that your content can be embedded in other users' profiles with appropriate widgets so that they, too, can share your library's innovative content.

Keep it up. Social network sites need regular care, as your profile will get new requests, mail, discussion board postings, and other items that require attention every day. Keep the content changing and interesting, and, with time, you will develop a community that will do much of your push marketing for you.

►5

BEST PRACTICES

- ► Follow Friending Etiquette
- ► Use Proper Tone, Language, and Content
- ► Blend the Professional with the Personal
- ► Engage in Reactive and Proactive Services

Social network sites exist as their own culture, one that blends together mainstream culture, youth culture, geek culture, and pop culture. With all of these forces intermingling, it can become confusing for someone new to these sites. This chapter will help you understand basic etiquette and the best methods for having an excellent experience with a social network site.

► FOLLOW FRIENDING ETIQUETTE

Friending, the act of making a connection between two profiles, is managed in three general ways. The first group of individuals only friend those they know. This group is less likely to add as a Friend those users they knew in a past context and who they have not stayed in touch with. The second group friends current and past contacts and might occasionally friend someone they have never met before. The third group will friend everyone they possibly can in an attempt to get as many Friend connections as possible (boyd, 2006). This is often the case with aspiring Internet celebrities, as well as individuals trying to market their latest book, Web site, or gadget. All three of these options are possible for libraries and librarians alike, but most libraries and librarians will find themselves falling into the second category.

As a librarian, it is up to you to decide who and how to add as a Friend. Most of your Friends will be individuals you know from everyday life. It is generally not a good idea to go out friending users and students randomly; this behavior can be seen as a form of spamming. Also, when friending another social network site user, it is good to send a note with the Friend request, clarifying how you know the person. Librarians are often unsure whether they should friend library users or students. It is often best to just let them friend you:

> However, this actually works out—students like counting faculty as their friends. If you've created a rich profile, it shows students that you care about [Facebook], and use it somewhat regularly. With the advent of news feeds, students will broadcast the fact they've [F]riended you, and this will start the friend requests coming in. (Stutzman, 2006)

This also allows users to dictate the relationship, preventing the librarian from seeming pushy or nosy. Because you do not have to add users as Friends to interact with them, you can still send users a private message or help them publicly through discussion boards and groups. Mentioning your Facebook account casually in conversation or during library workshops is a quick way to have folks add you as a Friend!

As a library, it is possible to add users as Friends first. Make sure to only perform Friend requests to those who use your library. It increases your chances of a successful Friend request if you send a personal note, explaining why you are requesting the person as a Friend. Depending on the user, this behavior will either be accepted or ignored—it is unlikely that the behavior will be reported as spam if you are not being deceptive or trying to sell something. By reaching out toward users in this way, you are able to proactively market directly to your users and develop an online relationship with them where they can get information about the library in a continuous way.

▶ USE PROPER TONE, LANGUAGE, AND CONTENT

The tone and language that you use on a social network site definitely sets the stage for future interactions. Because social network sites are characterized by familiarity and social relationships, it should not be surprising to see mostly informal language used. Library workers should not be distressed to see the occasional use of shorthand or SMS-style "text speak." However, it should also be noted that the use of proper spelling, grammar, and punctuation will not generally count against you! Presenting yourself and your library using informal (but correct) language will make both the library worker and the library itself more approachable.

Many social network site users are aware that they are participating in a public space online. A user's choice of public posts, comments on Friends' walls, and status updates are all immediately visible to that user's Friends. Because of this, wit, humor, and entertainment are all highly valued in the presentation of content. A library whose public actions on a social network site are interesting will draw attention: by presenting content in a novel, interesting, or funny way, you are sure to gather Friends more quickly.

Last, it is important to be genuine in your presentation of content. Users (especially younger users) are hypersensitive to language and can tell when they are being coaxed, manipulated, or pandered to. It is important to be honest in your dealings with users and not attempt to be disingenuous in an attempt to gather Friends. If you are marketing services that you don't believe in, users will be able to tell. When you are excited about your library, it will be easy to get your users excited about your library.

▶ BLEND THE PROFESSIONAL WITH THE PERSONAL

The advent of the social Web has brought about many changes, including the blurring between professional and personal lives. Library workers who are unfamiliar with social network sites may initially see them as online CVs (and, in the case of business sites, like LinkedIn, they would be mostly correct). However, the social nature of these sites means that they are designed to help site users connect with each other on a personal, social level. Although this can appear to conflict directly with the professional library world, it does not have to.

There are several options to deal with this tension between the personal and professional spheres of life. The first option is to leave the profile completely professional. By not including any personal information on the profile (interests, hobbies, contact information), you do not open that information up for comment by your Friends. However, this can often leave a profile looking sterile and will not encourage coworkers or users to engage you.

Second, you could keep your account completely personal and not engage in any work-related activity via social network sites. Many professionals choose this route, but it obviously prevents any sort of outreach to users.

The third option would be to keep separate accounts, one each for professional and personal life. Fifty-one percent of American adults on social network sites have more than one profile. Of these, 19 percent have multiple profiles to keep their professional and personal lives separate (Lenhart, 2009). If you have two profiles on the same site, it can generally be confusing for individuals who search for you. Also, it can leave both friends and coworkers feeling uneasy if they see that you have two accounts, one of which they aren't allowed to access.

Alternatively, you could create accounts on separate sites, as do 83 percent of adult social network site users (Lenhart, 2009). It would not be unusual to have a professional account on a business-oriented social network and a personal account on a more general social network. Again, however, refusing to interact socially with users via social network sites prevents any outreach you can do as a librarian; at the same time, refusing to add as a Friend coworkers on a social network site may bruise some egos at work.

Optionally, you can also make use of the social network site's privacy options to limit which information is visible to which users. This can be an excellent option for navigating the touchy space between personal and professional lives, but it can also require an investment of time. Rather than just accepting Friend requests as they come in, it requires you to select which information you would like that particular Friend to see. If you want to prevent your coworkers from seeing your relationship status, all you have to do is exclude that information from their view of your profile. You can do this in Facebook using Lists and in MySpace using Categories. Remember, however, that this is not an all-in-one solution. Information about you can always be "leaked" from one group to another (this is the social Web, after all).

Last, you can simply blend the personal and professional into a single social network site profile. Many librarians do this (myself included), as it allows them to connect with both users and coworkers on a personal level, while still maintaining professional contacts within the field. By adding personal status updates, taking quizzes, and posting pictures from social events and vacations, you present yourself as a whole person. This approach requires balance and common sense. Because your profile's audience will be a mixed group of personal and professional, it can take some time to find your own comfort zone between work and home life. Remember that any behavior posted online can be quickly spread around, so keep disparaging remarks about coworkers, drunken photographs, and other embarrassing way-too-realia offline! As stated before, if something is truly private, don't put it up on the Web in the first place.

▶ ENGAGE IN REACTIVE AND PROACTIVE SERVICES

Most of the services that the library offers are reactive services—they require that the library user take most of the steps in the information-seeking process. Users must, on their own:

- ▶ recognize that they have an information need;
- ▶ be able to formulate their information need in a clear and cogent manner;
- ▶ know the appropriate location, resource, or person to help answer that need;
- ▶ be able to find and understand the information; and
- ▶ be able to evaluate the information.

Because most users do not routinely perform advanced information searches, the requirement that they already know how a library works, or which person/desk to go to, can be intimidating, frustrating, and discouraging. Those lucky few who can successfully navigate their way to get help from a reference librarian are often amazed at the ease with which the librarian can find the information they need!

Social network sites offer an alternative method of service delivery—proactive service. Often, users may not be aware that they have an information need, or they may have no idea how to go about answering that need. In providing proactive service, librarians actively seek out users who have information needs and then give the users the opportunity to follow up on those information needs. Brian Mathews calls this being a "ubiquitous librarian." For example, Mathews (2007) joined a group for incoming freshmen on Facebook and answered their questions at the point of need:

> The students have responded favorably. At this phase their optimism is very high and they seem to like having a direct connection to the school. This illustrates the *ubiquitous* philosophy—that it doesn't always have to be about the books, journals, and library services. There is a time for that and this is not that time. For me it is more about fitting into the community, finding genuine needs, and helping out when possible. Student success involves more than peer-reviewed journal articles and proper citation style.

This can seem like a drastic departure from the traditional services that a library offers—and it is. Library workers have a tendency to answer questions only when directly asked.

Librarians often see this as a method of respecting the privacy of the user; if the librarians were to answer a question that was not *directed at them*, they would be invading that user's privacy. However, in the world of social media, questions are often directed at the community as a whole; these questions are in no way private or confidential. By answering questions that are directed to users in general, librarians are able to provide authoritative answers (with resources, to boot!) that would not have been available otherwise. Most social network site users are very aware of their privacy and will not pose sensitive or confidential questions in a public forum, whether online or offline.

It is not the responsibility of librarians to reach out into our communities to provide help where we can; however, it is a gift we can offer to our users. As part of the suite of Web 2.0 services out there, social network sites enable librarians to communicate directly with users on an even playing field. This is what Michael Stephens (2005) refers to when he describes the Library 2.0 principles: "The library is human [and] the library recognizes that its users are human too." By going beyond just trying to be approachable, and instead proactively approaching our users when they need us, we will be able to offer free, value-added services in ways they have never seen before.

▶6

MEASURES OF SUCCESS

- ▶ **Monitor Usage Statistics**
- ▶ **Take Surveys**
- ▶ **Hold Focus Groups**
- ▶ **Set and Achieve Goals**

Administrators, trustees, and the public often demand assessments to prove that library time and resources are being spent wisely. This is often a large challenge considering the budget restrictions that libraries face today. Luckily, many of the emerging technologies discussed in the Tech Set series come with tools that automatically collect and organize statistics for easy use. You can use any of the following techniques to gather both quantitative and qualitative statistics to measure your social network site presence, improve profiles, and give a voice to the profile's visitors.

▶ MONITOR USAGE STATISTICS

One of the most popular ways to perform assessment is to provide usage statistics for your library's profile. These statistics often include the profile's number of Friends, unique daily visitors, and how long someone stayed on your library's profile. Some social network sites automatically generate statistics and provide them to you. Others require you to install a piece of code (often called a **script**) onto the profile.

MySpace profile usage statistics can be recorded with an external analytics script. Because MySpace does not allow the placement of JavaScript in the user's profile, services like Google Analytics will not work. Instead, you can use free statistics Web sites that don't require JavaScript, such as StatCounter (www .statcounter.com) or StatSync (www.statsync.com). These Web sites will help you generate a script, which you can then paste into your profile. When you are ready to view your statistics, just log into the statistics Web site to view the results.

Facebook automatically records statistics for pages using the Insights tool. Insights measures the demographics of visitors to your library's page, including age, sex, and number of visits. In addition, it counts the number of page views, new and total Fans, user reviews, and user actions, such as photo views and wall posts. The Insights data can be downloaded as an XLS or CSV file for further manipulation in a spreadsheet program.

Statistics can be used when reporting success to administrators, but they can also be used to further improve the social network site profile. Does your profile get more traffic during a particular time of the week? Is it more popular with a certain age group? This information can be used to choose when to deploy content, as well as which content to include. Look carefully at the usage statistics gathered and take note of when different content is included on the profile. Does the profile get more traffic when a certain kind of content is included? By asking these questions, you can craft a profile that meets the interests of your users.

▶ TAKE SURVEYS

Surveys are a great way to learn what users want and what they need. By asking a series of carefully worded questions, you can discover your users' preferences, as well as their information needs. This is helpful not only for planning your library's social network site presence but also for continued assessment of that presence.

On an annual basis, ask visitors to your library's profile about their visit. These are some sample questions to include:

> ▶ What was the purpose of your visit to the library's profile today?

▶ Did you find the information that you needed?

▶ How often do you use the library's resources (including the physical library, the library's Web site, and the library's profile)?

▶ Which of these three do you use most often?

▶ What part of the library's profile do you find the most helpful?

▶ What part of the library's profile do you find the least helpful?

▶ What would you like to see added to the library's profile?

By asking questions regularly, you are allowing users to help you craft the social network site profile of their preference. Keeping the question user- and task-centered helps prevent the profile from growing into a librarian-centered tool. Some libraries may find that their users want more academic resources, while other libraries' users may want more social or entertainment resources. Taking surveys will help you to stay in touch with your users' needs while also providing them a voice to the administration.

▶ HOLD FOCUS GROUPS

Focus groups can be a quite revealing way to gather qualitative data about your library's social network site presence. By gathering together users who have friended your library and by allowing them to interact while discussing the library's profile, you can acquire detailed data about their preferences.

Focus groups can be conducted in person or online. For in-person focus groups, it is best to have a moderator who is not associated with the library or its social network site presence. You can often recruit volunteer moderators from psychology or sociology graduate student interns at local colleges or universities. Draft a series of open-ended questions that you would like to see answered. Make sure to provide incentives to compensate participants for their time—gift certificates to local stores, small prizes, and food are often successful. Provide two available dates, and invite Friends via the social network site to participate. Each focus group should have between 5 and 15 participants.

Online focus groups are another viable option, especially for discussions focusing around online tools. Participants can gather in an online chat room by using free Web sites such as DimDim (www.dimdim.com), Yugma (www.yugma.com), or Vyew (http://vyew.com). These online meeting services allow users to chat in real-time and also allow users to view the library's profile at the same time. Again, the same guidelines for in-person focus groups apply.

▶ SET AND ACHIEVE GOALS

It is important to use the measurements you gather to improve the library's profile. It is tempting to leave assessment until the last minute and then include whatever is available in the mandatory annual or quarterly report. However, the information that you gather will be valuable to the continued success of your social network site outreach. By giving the users what they want and need, you will be able to not only serve your regular library users but also reach out to a whole new audience!

Set modest, measurable goals for your library's presence on the social network site. These goals can be quantitative, such as increasing unique views or numbers of Friends; or it can be qualitative, such as seeking positive comments or reviews. The purpose of these goals is not to judge the immediate success or failure of the library's profile but to give milestones for the creation and growth of the service.

Also, do not become disheartened if your statistics do not jump overnight. Remember that your profile will not be perfect or popular the instant that it is created. It can often take over a year before your profile will see steady usage. It is important during this growing time to continue to include interesting and up-to-date information via your library's profile. As you do so, you will see the numbers slowly rise!

GLOSSARY

add: Short for "adding as a Friend." As in, "Thanks for the add!" *See* FRIENDING.

app: *See* APPLICATION.

application: A small program designed to work within a social network site. Facebook applications (or apps) will only work on the Facebook site. Applications have a variety of purposes, including communication, entertainment, and research.

API: An application programming interface (API) is a set of rules and procedures used to create applications. An API is often described by restricting the language in which the application is written.

CAPTCHA: A security measure in computing consisting of a challenge-response test. By identifying text or audio, the user proves that he or she is not a computer. CAPTCHAs are used to prevent spam and the creation of fake accounts on social network sites.

chat aggregator: A program that allows a user to log in to multiple instant messaging services at once, such as MSN Messenger, Yahoo Messenger, AOL Instant Messenger, MySpace IM, and Facebook Chat. Examples of chat aggregator programs include Pidgin, Adium, Trillian, Meebo, and Fire.

Facebook: A social network site that became famous for being popular with college students. As of May 2009, it is globally the most popular social network site.

Fan: In Facebook, a Fan is a user who has created a relationship between his or her profile and a Facebook page. This displays the user's interest in, association with, or approval of the subject of the Facebook page.

Friend: A Friend is someone with whom a social network site user has created a profile connection. This does not imply friendship in everyday life but instead shows that the two users are connected in some way. These connections can be either weak or strong, depending on the relationship the two users have.

friending: The act of creating a connection between your profile and another user's profile. As in, "Thanks for friending me!"

Friendster: A social network site founded in 2002 that quickly gained popularity, but then lost its popularity with U.S. users after it had severe connection problems. It has since gained a sizeable market in Asia.

invite: To use a social network site's built-in feature to send an invitation (aka "an invite") to another user to join the site.

Library 2.0: A philosophy of library service that leverages emerging technologies to provide collaborative, user-centered design in the creation and delivery of content and services.

LinkedIn: A business-oriented social network site that was launched in 2003 and now has over 40 million users.

MySpace: A social network site that became famous for being popular with youth and as a venue for discovering new music. As of May 2009, it is globally the second most popular social network site.

network: In Facebook, networks are schools, businesses, or geographical areas that users can associate with. For privacy, some information within Facebook is only viewable by other users within the same network. Users can belong to more than one network at a time.

Ning: A Web site used to create distinct social network sites by and for communities. Each social network site is identified by its subdomain. For example, the Library 2.0 Ning site is located at http://library20.ning.com.

OpenSocial: A Web standard and API for the creation and use of applications and social data across different Web sites (such as

MySpace, Orkut, and iGoogle). OpenSocial is used to create MySpace apps.

page: In Facebook, a page is a profile for a nonhuman entity. Libraries, businesses, ideas, and public figures can all have pages to represent them.

plug-in: A small computer program that works with a larger Web site to perform a specific function. Unlike applications and widgets, which allow Web site visitors to interact with content, plug-ins are typically behind-the-scenes and invisible to users.

profile: An online representation of a person or institution. Individuals use their profiles to publicly connect to real-life and online social networks.

script: *See* WIDGET.

social network: A social structure made up of individuals who are connected to one another through different forms of social relationships.

social network site: A Web site that allows users to (1) create a profile, (2) connect their profile to that of other users, and (3) view and explore the connections between profiles.

social networking: (1) The act of meeting new individuals and expanding your social network in the process. (2) The name used by popular media for social network sites.

social Web: Web sites that allow users to interact with one another around the content of the Web site.

viral: When a video, Web site, or other form of online media spreads quickly through a social network like a virus, through the power of the media's popularity.

Web 2.0: An array of Web-based services that connect users to each other. Examples include social network sites, instant messaging, blogs, microblogs, wikis, podcasts, vidcasts, and social bookmark sites.

widget: HTML code that is inserted into a social network site profile or Web page to import content from a separate page. Widgets are used to embed content from external blogs, photo-sharing sites, video-sharing sites, etc.

▶ RECOMMENDED RESOURCES

▶ INTRODUCTORY VIDEO

CommonCraft: Social Networking in Plain English
www.commoncraft.com/video-social-networking

The CommonCraft Web site includes explanatory videos on a variety of topics, including wikis, Twitter, social bookmarking, and even zombies! This two-minute video on social network sites gives a quick introduction to the topic, explaining the value of the sites and the basic mechanics of how they work. The Web site allows you to e-mail the video to others so that you can quickly and easily introduce others to the concepts behind social network sites.

▶ SCHOLARLY RESEARCHERS

danah boyd
www.danah.org

danah boyd (no capitalization by her own choice) is a researcher and scholar in the field of social network sites; she received her PhD from the University of California at Berkeley's School of Information. Specifically, she researches how teenagers interact in networked public sites like MySpace, YouTube, and Twitter. Her research has been foundational to the academic study of social network sites, and she will doubtlessly continue to be a leader in this field. You can find her publications at the above address, or you can read her blog at www.zephoria .org/thoughts.

Alice Marwick

www.tiara.org

Alice Marwick, PhD candidate at New York University in the Department of Media, Culture, and Communication, researches a variety of social software topics, including blogs (especially LiveJournal), social network sites, and the relationship between technology and society. Her dissertation work is on social media and how it affects status.

Fred Stutzman

http://fstutzman.com

A PhD candidate at UNC Chapel Hill's School of Information and Library Science, Fred Stutzman studies social technologies and their use by different populations. He is noted for speaking and writing on the intersection of social media and education, an area of intense interest to librarians. His Web site is Unit Structures—Fred Stutzman's thoughts about information, social networks and technology.

▶ SOCIAL NETWORK SITE NEWS

All Facebook: The Unofficial Facebook Blog

www.allfacebook.com

The All Facebook blog is a third-party blog that covers developments at Facebook, including new services and applications, business deals, and tensions between Facebook and its users. Because Facebook is the clear leader of worldwide social network sites, it is valuable to read about developments from an outsider that aren't posted on the official Facebook blog.

Mashable: The Social Media Guide

http://mashable.com

Mashable is a site that aggregates news and information about social media. It is well-known for its giant lists on a variety of topics (such as "Facebook Powertools: 150+ Apps, Scripts and Add-Ons for Facebook"). It also serves as a clearinghouse for developing stories on the changing landscape of social media. MySpace and Facebook are covered in detail, alongside Bebo, Friendster, YouTube, and Flickr.

▶ LIBRARIES AND TECHNOLOGY

LibrarianInBlack

http://librarianinblack.typepad.com

Sarah Houghton-Jan has one of the longest-running librarian blogs. She keeps her readers abreast of the latest developments in a variety of library-related topics. She is notable for introducing librarians to new and interesting technologies that can make an impact on our ability to serve users. As a talented speaker, consultant, and writer on technology in libraries, Houghton-Jan's blog includes her presentation materials, enabling users to keep up with changes and new tools in this sphere.

Library 2.0 Ning

http://library20.ning.com

The Library 2.0 network on Ning is a grassroots effort by library workers to interact and learn about this evolving concept and its impact on libraries. The site is a useful place to start exploring many of the tools of the social Web and their impact on libraries. Library workers will find this a welcome place to ask questions and get answers from other frontline staff.

Tame the Web: Libraries, Technology & People

http://tametheweb.com

Dr. Michael Stephens is Associate Professor of Library and Information Science at Dominican University, and his blog Tame the Web serves as an aggregator for a lot of progressive thought about libraries and technology. As one of the leading proponents of Library 2.0, Stephens' blog pulls together original posts, guest articles, and thoughtful commentary. Topics include the role of technology in libraries, the relationships among library workers, users, and administration, and the policies that affect developments in these areas.

REFERENCES AND FURTHER READING

Alexa Internet. "Alexa Top 500 Global Sites." Alexa Internet, Inc. (May 26, 2009). Available: www.alexa.com/topsites (accessed December 16, 2009).

American Library Association. "YALSA Compiles Resources for Librarians about Online Social Networking." Chicago: American Library Association (August 8, 2006). Available: www.ala.org/ala/newspresscenter/news/pressreleases2006/august2006/yalsaonlinenetworkingres.cfm (accessed December 16, 2009).

"book rental service?" Overclockers Australia Forums (January 29, 2008). Available: http://forums.overclockers.com.au/showthread.php?t=648654 (accessed December 16, 2009).

boyd, danah. 2006. "Friends, Friendsters, and Top 8: Writing Community into Being on Social Network Sites." *First Monday* 11, no. 12 (December 4). Available: http://firstmonday.org/htbin/cgiwrap/bin/ojs/index.php/fm/article/view/1418/1336 (accessed December 16, 2009).

———. 2007. "Why Youth (Heart) Social Network Sites: The Role of Networked Publics in Teenage Social Life." In *MacArthur Foundation Series on Digital Learning—Youth, Identity, and Digital Media Volume,* edited by David Buckingham. Cambridge, MA: MIT Press, p. 14. Available: www.danah.org/papers/WhyYouthHeart.pdf (accessed December 16, 2009).

boyd, danah m. and Nicole B. Ellison. 2007. "Social Network Sites: Definition, History, and Scholarship." *Journal of Computer-Medi-*

ated Communication 13, no. 1, article 11. Available: http://jcmc
.indiana.edu/vol13/issue1/boyd.ellison.html (accessed December 16, 2009).

Brown, Jim. "MySpace as a Teaching Tool." Blogging Pedagogy
(November 27, 2006). Available: http://pedagogy.cwrl.utexas
.edu/node/162 (accessed December 16, 2009).

comScore. "More Than Half of MySpace Visitors Are Now Age 35
or Older, as the Site's Demographic Composition Continues to
Shift." comScore, Inc. (October 5, 2006). Available: www
.comscore.com/esl/Press_Events/Press_Releases/2006/10/
More_than_Half_MySpace_Visitors_Age_35 (accessed December 16, 2009).

Doucett, Elisabeth. 2009. *Creating Your Library Brand.* Chicago:
ALA Editions.

Drew, Bill. "Facebook Closing Organization Pages Such as Libraries" (August 25, 2006). Available: http://babyboomerlibrarian
.blogspot.com/2006/08/facebook-closing-organization-pages
.html (accessed December 16, 2009).

Dunbar, R.I.M. 1993. "Coevolution of Neocortical Size, Group Size
and Language in Humans." *Behavioral and Brain Sciences* 16, no.
4: 681–735.

Ellison, Nicole B., Charles Steinfield, and Cliff Lampe. 2007. "The
Benefits of Facebook 'Friends': Social Capital and College Students' Use of Online Social Network Sites." *Journal of Com-
puter-Mediated Communication* 12, no. 4. Available: http://jcmc
.indiana.edu/vol12/issue4/ellison.html (accessed December
16, 2009).

Facebook Login. Available: www.facebook.com/s.php?q=library+
catalog+search (accessed December 16, 2009).

Hampton, K. and B. Wellman. 2003. "Neighboring in Netville:
How the Internet Supports Community and Social Capital in a
Wired Suburb." *City and Community* 2, no. 4: 277–311. Available:
www.chass.utoronto.ca/~wellman/publications/neighboring/
neighboring_netville.pdf (accessed December 16, 2009).

Houghton-Jan, Sarah. "IL 2006: MySpace & Facebook" (October
24, 2006). Available: http://librarianinblack.net/librarianin

black/2006/10/il_2006_myspace.html (accessed December 16, 2009).

Landis, Cliff. 2007. "Connecting to Users with Facebook." Georgia Library Quarterly 43, no. 4 (Winter): 6.

Lee, Ellen. 2007. "MySpace Suit Dismissed by Judge in Texas: Family Said Site Didn't Protect Underage Users." San Francisco Chronicle, February 15: C-2. Available: www.sfgate.com (accessed December 16, 2009).

Lenhart, Amanda. "Adults and Social Network Websites." Pew Internet & American Life Project (January 14, 2009). Available: www.pewinternet.org/Reports/2009/Adults-and-Social-Network -Websites.aspx (accessed December 16, 2009).

Lenhart, Amanda, and Mary Madden. "Social Networking Websites and Teens: An Overview." Pew Internet & American Life Project (January 7, 2007). Available: www.pewinternet.org/ Reports/2007/Social-Networking-Websites-and-Teens.aspx (accessed December 16, 2009).

Marketing Week. "In the World of 'Pull,' Push the Facts, and the Product Will Sell." Marketing Week (July 20, 2006): 26. Available: www.marketingweek.co.uk (accessed December 16, 2009).

Marwick, Alice. 2008. "To Catch a Predator: The MySpace Moral Panic. First Monday 13, no. 6. Available: www.uic.edu/htbin/ cgiwrap/bin/ojs/index.php/fm/article/view/2152/1966 (accessed December 16, 2009).

Mathews, Brian. "Making a Good First Impression: Facebook & Incoming Freshmen" (July 2, 2007). Available: http:// theubiquitouslibrarian.typepad.com/the_ubiquitous_librarian/ 2007/07/making-a-good-f.html (accessed December 16, 2009).

O'Neill, Nick. "Facebook Opens Status API, Say Goodbye to Twitter." All Facebook: The Unofficial Facebook Resource (February 6, 2009). Available: www.allfacebook.com/2009/02/ facebook-opens-status-api-say-goodbye-to-twitter/ (accessed December 16, 2009).

Ostrow, Adam. "Breaking: Facebook Announces Ad Network Plans" (November 6, 2007). Available: http://mashable

.com/2007/11/06/facebook-ads/ (accessed December 16, 2009).

Preston, Leandra. 2008. "A Space of Our Own: MySpace and Feminist Activism in the Classroom." *Radical Teacher* 81: 14–19.

Rainey, Lee. "Friending Libraries: Why Libraries Can Become Nodes in People's Social Networks." Pew Internet & American Life Project (March 30, 2009). Available: www.pewinternet .org/Presentations/2009/8-Friending-libraries.aspx (accessed December 16, 2009).

Reuters. "MySpace Deletes 29,000 Sex Offenders" (July 24, 2007). Available: www.reuters.com/article/idUSN2424879820070724 (accessed December 16, 2009).

Rosen, Larry D. 2006. "Adolescents in MySpace: Identity Formation, Friendship and Sexual Predators." Available: www .csudh.edu/psych/Adolescents%20in%20MySpace%20-%20 Executive%20Summary.pdf (accessed December 16, 2009).

Siess, Judith A. 2003. *The Visible Librarians: Asserting Your Value with Marketing and Advocacy.* Chicago: American Library Association.

Smith, Justin. "Number of US Facebook Users Over 35 Nearly Doubles in the Last 60 Days" (March 25, 2009). Available: www.insidefacebook.com/2009/03/25/number-of-us-facebook -users-over-35-nearly-doubles-in-last-60-days/ (accessed December 16, 2009).

Stephens, Michael. *The Collected Principles of Library 2.0 for Pondering* (December 7, 2005). Available: http://tametheweb.com/ 2005/12/the_collected_principles_of_li.html (accessed December 16, 2009).

———. *Web 2.0 & Libraries: Best Practices for Social Software* (July/August 2006). Available: www.alatechsource.org/ltr/web-20-and-libraries-best-practices-for-social-software (accessed December 4, 2009).

———. "Exploring the Virtual Commons: Using Ning to Build a Community at Lafayette Public Library." ALA TechSource (March 5, 2009). Available: www.alatechsource.org/blog/ 2009/03/exploring-the-virtual-commons-using-ning-to-build-a-community-at-lafayette-public-libra (accessed December 16, 2009).

Stone, Brad. "New Tool from Facebook Extends Its Web Presence." *New York Times,* July 24, 2008. Available: www.nytimes.com/2008/07/24/technology/24facebook.html?_r=1 (accessed December 16, 2009).

Stutzman, Fred. "Facebook as a Tool for Learning Engagement" (December 20, 2006). Available: http://chimprawk.blogspot.com/2006/12/facebook-as-tool-for-learning.html (accessed December 16, 2009).

Tennant, Roy. 2006. "The Library Brand." *Library Journal* (January 15, 2006). Available: http://roytennant.com/column/?fetch=data/22.xml (accessed December 16, 2009).

Watershed Publishing. "Older Users Help Facebook Grow 149% in February." Watershed Publishing, Inc. Available: www.marketingcharts.com/interactive/older-users-help-facebook-grow-149-in-february-8602/ (accessed December 16, 2009).

Willard, Nancy. "Research That Is 'Outdated and Inadequate'? An Analysis of the Pennsylvania Child Predator Unit Arrests in Response to Attorney General Criticism of the Berkman Task Force Report." Center for Safe and Responsible Internet Use (January 26, 2009). Available: http://csriu.org/PDFs/papredator.pdf (accessed December 16, 2009).

Yadav, Sid. "Facebook—The Complete Biography." Mashable (August 25, 2006). Available: http://mashable.com/2006/08/25/facebook-profile/ (accessed December 16, 2009).

INDEX

Page numbers followed by the letter "f" indicate figures.

ABOUT THE AUTHOR

Cliff Landis is Technology Librarian at Valdosta State University in Valdosta, Georgia. He received his bachelor's degree in Religious Studies and Philosophy from Auburn University in 2002 and his master's degree in Library and Information Science from Florida State University in 2004.

Cliff joined his first social network site in 2001 and has since been active on dozens of different sites, connecting with friends, evaluating services, and furthering his career as a professional geek. He has spoken nationally and internationally on a variety of library technology topics and is known for writing and presenting on social network sites, user-centric services, usability studies, the evolution of technology, and the future of libraries.

Cliff's research and scholarly interests spread across disciplines as he explores the connections between different fields and media. He can be found blogging at http://clifflandis.net.